FORGIVENESS THERAPY:

When Forgiveness Is the Only Cure.

*Based on a true story of how I forgave
the killers of my father.*

DR. CHARLES KARUKU.

Forgiveness Therapy

Copyright © 2017 by Institute of Leadership and Mentorship
Published 2017. Exponential Group Publishing
6720 E. Fowler Ave; Ste. 161 Tampa, Fl. 33617

Cover Graphics by Lindsey Karuku
Book Layout by Exponential Group Publishing

ISBN - 13: 978-1548439071
ISBN - 10: 154843907X

TABLE OF CONTENT

PREFACE

I t is not every day you find someone who had their father killed six months prior to their birth.

That's my story. I was thrust into a world of circumstances I never wished, planned or chose to come to. From day one of my life, there were only two options; live with bitterness the rest of my life or forgive and thrive past my pain to a better future. The choice was not communicated to me on day one. Until later in life, looking back with a 20-20 vision, I could see clearly where fate thrust me into. I was literally thrown into a household where my birth was received with both sighs of joy and tears of grief. I was one more orphan added on an already overloaded and sorrow stricken family. Growing up looking for a closure, the choice was finally presented decades later; forgive the killers of my father and find a closure, or else. I wrestled with this decision much more because I felt justified to be angry and bitter. But it was time to put this matter to rest. Four decades without a closure is a day too many. This is my story. This story is true and very unique.

The power of any story is found in its uniqueness. A unique story is like a DNA. It's one of a kind. It doesn't look like anything you've ever seen. That's what makes it unique. No two stories are alike. My story is my own just like the way I own my DNA. I promise you that behind this story is a power that will cause you to experience incredible transformation. You will understand and appreciate forgiveness probably more than you've ever done before.

The unique story is as unique as your fingerprints. It helps you put a mark in the world that cannot be erased. It is your contribution that is left for generations after you're gone. This story is my unique contribution to inspire others. That is why I felt compelled to tell it. Many people have heard me testify about how I forgave the killers of my father. Some have asked me to consider writing a book. The day has come. The book is here. I wrote it in an easy to read, down to earth style. I know a lot of lives will be touched as they read my unique story.

May this book serve as an inspiration for you too. May you too, find the courage to use your unique story for a positive contribution.

PROLOGUE

"Lord, make me an instrument of thy peace.

Where there is hatred, let me sow love;

Where there is injury, pardon;

Where there is doubt, faith;

Where there is despair, hope;

Where there is darkness, light;

Where there is sadness, joy.

O Divine Master, grant that I may not so much seek

To be consoled as to console,

To be understood as to understand,

To be loved as to love;

For it is in giving that we receive;

It is in pardoning that we are pardoned;

It is in dying to self that we are born to eternal life."

(Prayer of St. Francis of Assisi, 13th Century).

DEDICATION

First and foremost, I thank God for a book that comes from my heart. I pray this book may please God in every way.

To Lindsey, the most Godly woman anyone can ever find. She's a jewel and a solid rock in my life. Her tenacity and steadfastness are like wind underneath my wings. Finding you has given me feathers to help me fly further. I love you now even more than any words can express.

My mom, Miriam who taught me how to pray and have faith in God. Her tenacity and unshakable faith has given me a resilience that is priceless. It's become what I'm known for around the world. What a treasured inheritance!

My dad whom I never met, but everyone tells me I resemble him in so many good ways. I can feel the mantle of my father and the redemption of his legacy. My journey to find closure of his death led me to this revelation. His legacy lives on.

I also dedicate this work to my grandfather Joshua (of blessed memory) whose prophetic prayers have been answered through me. His legacy has given me something to pass on to the next generation.

My children Miriam, Israel, Jehu, Jemimah, and Phoebe. You're my ultimate dream come true. I've always wanted to inspire you. May this book be a way for me to give you broad shoulders on which to stand tall and aim higher. You're my legacy, and I love you dearly.

And to International Outreach Church, you're the people I've dedicated my sweat, blood, and tears. I can proudly say I've found my purpose through the privilege of serving with you. With profound gratitude, I say a big THANK YOU!

ACKNOWLEDGEMENT

I would like to register my appreciation to the many people whose contribution and inspiration made this book a reality. I thank those who helped, granted interviews, read, wrote, offered comments, allowed me to quote their remarks and assisted in the editing, proofreading, and design. Lindsey Karuku, thank you for doing your due diligence to put together an awesome cover design. For my kids, thank you for allowing dad to take time and complete this project within his self-imposed deadline.

You graciously endured this long and difficult time.

Thank you, Dr. LaJun Cole, for the inspiring word and leadership in my publishing process. Thank you, Dr. Amb. Clyde Rivers for always helping me and others to reach to the moon. This book has been a great dream come true. You and many others that I could not mention are my ultimate dream team. So many of you have waited for my book release. Here it is! Thank you.

INTRODUCTION

"Forgive by choice, not by feeling"
(Dr. Charles)

Many people struggle with forgiveness. I totally understand. I meet people every day who have had bad business relationships, bad marriages, bad breakups, mean-spirited relatives, neighbors, and friends who won't let up on hurting them. Whole nations and people groups have gone to war due to unresolved conflicts. The cost has been a countless loss of life and trillions of dollars down the drain. But at the root of all the personal or international chaos and conflicts, is people who won't allow forgiveness to work. It is my belief that every single problem on the earth that pertains to personal or national relationships can be resolved with the right measure of forgiveness.

Many years ago, I visited a family that had gone through a divorce. My pastoral visit happened at a time when their child was under a court-ordered joint custody. That night, this child was being transferred from one parent to the other. I witnessed the drama play out between the two ex-spouses who were so bitter with each other. None of them wanted to face the other. I witnessed the child refuse to leave the house to go spend the weekend with the other parent. I watched helplessly as the child fought, with kicking and screaming and not wanting to leave the house. Finally, the mother pushed the child out through the door to go and be with the father. The child screamed helplessly before disappearing to the father's vehicle. The mother came back crying and displaying all the bitterness of the experience that had become like a weekly reply of a horror movie.

Right there and then, my eyes were opened to the horrible experiences that some divorced families go through every day. It is the problem of having to deal with an ex-spouse that is still bitter and vindictive. That is where I began thinking about how to forgive someone when I don't feel like it. The thought occurred to me like an epiphany. There has to be a way to forgive people who don't deserve it.

Over the years I have counseled couples who have had an affair. That is what many people call the ultimate betrayal. As I counsel them, it is very difficult for whoever has had an affair to comfort the other spouse of the pain that they have caused through their betrayal. I have found myself over and over again, reminding those people that forgiveness is a choice and not a feeling.

I wrote this book to people who have gone through pain, failure, shame, humiliation, bitter divorce, affairs, betrayal, breakups, and all kinds of destructive relationships. I was thinking the other day about narcissists. As some of you may know, the most difficult divorce is the one that comes from a narcissist. This is a person who is completely self-absorbed and cares for no one but themselves. They lack even the tiniest iota of compassion or even a little trace of grace. They're mean, egocentric and ego maniacs. Their words and actions are laced with the venom of vindictiveness and meanness. Their priority is to serve and protect the three main people in their lives; the me, the myself and the I. They normally leave their ex-spouse/lover completely devastated, destroyed, hurt beyond repair and left for the dead. Since narcissists are cold and calculating, they like to leave their victim suddenly by using the element of surprise. They know how to set their victims up for the greatest trauma and devastation. In most times, the narcissist leaves their victim unexpectedly for another person. This causes them to hate themselves. They use rejection, abandonment and ultimate betrayal as a weapon to destroy their victims. Many people who come out of those kinds of relationships never heal. They are totaled, traumatized, destroyed and hurt almost to the point of beyond repair.

Many narcissists will never allow their ex-lovers to go unpunished. The divorce or breakup may also ruin them financially. Divorce from a narcissist has the potential to fatally cripple their victim emotionally and mentally. I have met countless people who have been divorced for years. Unfortunately, most of them are still languishing in their pain and trapped by the trauma. Some of them embrace the pain, and they live with it. We see it in the choices they make after the divorce. Some of them make an inner vow that they will never ever trust or be married again. Others decide to become homosexuals or lesbians. The others make the conclusion that all men or all women are evil.

There is a difference between acting and reacting. I wrote this book to help everyone get totally healed and also heal properly. I believe this book will help you and your loved ones heal to the deepest cuts and wounds. God wants you to act and not react. Learning how to forgive is the best way to act proactively as far as your life is concerned.

Always remember success is summoned when you decide to live by principle. The principle of forgiveness opens doors to the most exciting way of life that you'll ever discover. It allows you to live a happy and fulfilled life. Always allow people to be people. Never yield your power to those willing to control you and swing your emotions at their whims. At the end of the day, you cannot make people do anything. Neither can you change people. People have to have their choices and live their life as they please. That is something you cannot control. The only person, the only choice and the only change you can successfully make is on yourself.

Let's face some hard facts. The truth is that as long as you walk, live and talk you will be offended. Forgiveness is not something that you deal with once and never have to do it again. It's not one of those once in a lifetime deal, like being born out of your mother's womb. It is something that has to become a way of life. Every day you will use forgiveness in dealing with toxic people, negative people, bitter/angry people, family, friends, spouses, children, employees, business partners, neighbors, other drivers on the highway, and old enemies. Walking in forgiveness is the key to living a happy life in this world.

I have observed time after time people self-sabotage with negative behaviors that are consistent with predictable outcomes. Most of those outcomes are self-destructive. To watch a good person self-destruct is like watching an accident waiting to happen. I wrote this book because I believe in the power of forgiveness. I have seen how self-destructive unforgiveness has been to too many people. I can confidently say that most of the people issues I deal with can be resolved with a simple act of forgiveness.

For me, forgiveness is a very personal journey. I wrote this book because I have lived on both sides of the choices. I don't claim to be the flawless expert on this subject. However, I have learned enough lessons, and hopefully, I can help you get a grip on some of the issues that you've been dealing with. Finally, the eternal benefits of passing the test of forgiveness is when you enter into the most wonderful and fulfilling way of life you've ever had. I am here to tell you that all things are possible. Step into your destiny. See you at the top of your mountain!

PROACTIVE FORGIVENESS.

LEARN TO PRACTICE PROACTIVE FORGIVENESS OTHER THAN REACTIVE FORGIVENESS

Proactive forgiveness is by design. Reactive forgiveness is a knee-jerk reaction, and it's normally by default.

The word proactive means to prepare for, intervene in or control an expected occurrence or situation, especially a negative or difficult one. It requires that we anticipate. As a result, we are intentional about creating or controlling the situation by causing something to happen rather than responding to it after it has happened.

Proactive forgiveness moves past having head knowledge of why we forgive to actually doing it. It also involves intervention to help silence the mouth of the accuser and stop the drip drip of joy, peace, and blessings.

Throughout our lives, we will all be faced with situations when we are wronged, hurt, or even abused; and yet we must decide to forgive. You might consciously know all of the incredible benefits of forgiveness, but what if you're just not there yet? What if you understand all the benefits but still don't feel like forgiving? That's when we use proactive forgiveness.

God has promised to answer our prayers speedily. But many people do not see that. Are you experiencing too much obstruction? Frustrated prayer life? Strongholds that won't fall? Are you at a point where you feel like you've done all you can?

Are you dealing with some long-standing strongholds? Unanswered prayers? Cycles of oppression, delays, unusual obstructions and strange warfare? Maybe you need to reexamine your heart and see what is going on in the realm of forgiveness.

Unforgiveness could be your obstruction: It can be the cause of many sicknesses, unanswered prayers, hindrances, tormenting spirits and accusations of the enemy in your intercession.

MOUNTAIN MOVING FAITH IS MEANT TO ALWAYS WORK. BUT UNFORGIVENESS HINDERS IT.

[22]"Have faith in God," Jesus answered. [23]"Truly I tell you, if anyone says to this mountain, 'Go, throw yourself into the sea,' and does not doubt in their heart but believes that what they say will happen, it will be done for them. [24]Therefore I tell you, whatever you ask for in prayer, believe that you have received it, and it will be

yours. [25]And when you stand praying, if you hold anything against anyone, forgive them, so that your Father in heaven may forgive you your sins."

UNFORGIVENESS IS A HINDRANCE TO PRAYER.

1 Peter 3:7-Likewise, ye husbands, dwell with *them* according to knowledge, giving honor unto the wife, as unto the weaker vessel, and as being heirs together of the grace of life; that your prayers be not hindered.

UNFORGIVENESS CAN BE THE REASON FOR REJECTED OFFERINGS.

Matt 5:

[23]"Therefore, if you are offering your gift at the altar and there remember that your brother or sister has something against you, [24]leave your gift there in front of the altar. First, go and be reconciled to them; then come and offer your gift.

[25]"Settle matters quickly with your adversary who is taking you to court. Do it while you are still together on the way, or your adversary may hand you over to the judge, and the judge may hand you over to the officer, and you may be thrown into prison. [26]Truly I tell you, you will not get out until you have paid the last penny.

THE ENEMY WILL USE ALL THE LEGAL GROUND OF UNFORGIVENESS TO BUILD A STRONGHOLD.

Eph 4:27-Give no room to the devil.

FORGIVE BY CHOICE.

John 20- Whoever you forgive will be forgiven. Whoever you hold will be held. Learn to forgive with the help of the HS.

[21] Again Jesus said, "Peace be with you! As the Father has sent me, I am sending you." [22] And with that, he breathed on them and said, "Receive the Holy Spirit. [23] If you forgive anyone's sins, their sins are forgiven; if you do not forgive them, they are not forgiven."

Let me know how this book blesses your life and if it ends up changing you like it has done to me.

Sincerely,

Dr. Charles Karuku
Feb 2017.
Burnsville USA.

CHAPTER 1

MY 42 YEAR JOURNEY OF FORGIVENESS. HOW I FINALLY FORGAVE MY FATHER'S KILLERS.

"Unforgiveness is like taking poison and then expecting it to kill your enemy"
(Nelson Mandela)

The year was 1970. America was going through the turmoil of the Vietnam war. Richard Nixon had just gotten into office. But 8,000 miles away, my family was going through the beginning of their four-decade nightmare. It was in 1970 that my father was murdered in cold blood. It was a very painful death, especially for my siblings. My mom and my dad had just been married for only nine years when my father died. The oldest sibling was only nine years old.

It was not easy to have five orphaned children walking around in tattered clothes, and a mother fighting to hold herself together. Talk about trauma. Everyone was going through it. My father's sudden death had produced a widow and five orphans without any notice. Death always comes at the worst of times. My father had just bought a farm and started a business. He had not even paid off the farm. His name is Joseph. As a former freedom fighter and a liberator of the nation, my father's warrior instincts never left him. Having been a veteran guerrilla warrior for years, he had a side of him that was ready to fight. He was a mid-sized man, excellent accordion player, and a self-taught veterinarian. He was a total goofball on one hand and a short fuse on the other. My guess is that he struggled with Post Traumatic Stress Disorder. He used to drink heavily and was kind of a mean drunk. He was also very short tempered and tended to use violence under the least provocation.

He was only 35, smart, strong, ambitious, very zealous and burning with passion. His juices were full. He was finally stepping into the prime of his life. One night, he picked up a bar brawl (like it had happened so many times prior). A single kick through his forehead spelled doom to an ambitious man with a whole future in front of him. There he was. A life cut short. An ambition silenced. A man oozing with zeal and energy had finally been silenced. Death had done it again. It had snatched the best and most blooming flower in the vast garden called earth. All that was left were memories of loss, grief, endless emptiness and a sense of utter helplessness. My father was lost. Lost, lost, lost forever. He did not die alone. It seemed like he had died with a piece of each of us. For the first few years, it looked like he had taken away our future with him to a land where people never come back. It seemed like all the glimpse of hope and our identity was gone. Some neighbors wrote us off. As the obituary was read, it looked like they were reading the closing chapter of our entire family. Little did we know that it was just the beginning of a new chapter full of hopes, dreams, and aspirations on one side. But the other side of the chapter was a juxtaposition of pain, fear, grief, trauma and bare knuckle survival as we struggled to heal and move on.

To top it off, when my father died they were not aware that my widowed mom was pregnant with me. Three months after the funeral my mother discovered she was pregnant. Faced with a daunting task of bringing up six orphans, it seemed like all hope was gone. That is the world in which I was born. Very unpredictable, very chaotic and dreadful.

It was a few days to the end of 1970. The day was Tuesday of December 22, just 3 days before Christmas. My mother was working her tail off on the farm trying to make ends meet. Suddenly a pain shot through her stomach, then to her back, and then to her entire lower abdomen. She realized she was going into labor. She had no insurance or vehicle to take her to the doctor. She walked slowly to her dirt-floored shack, which we called our home. She sent for a neighbor lady to come and help deliver her baby. All African women had mastered this art of birthing for thousands of years. The craft of midwifing the birth of newborns had been passed down from generation to generation. All that the midwife needed was clean hands and a brand new razor blade to cut the umbilical chord. A few hours after the arrival of the neighbor lady, the water broke.

I was born on a dirt floor without a doctor or a nurse in the room. Only a neighbor lady with a razor blade to cut the umbilical chord. I arrived into the world at the most unpredictable times. Growing up with four brothers and two sisters my biggest question was, where is my father? I had no idea what had happened to him. A few years later I was big enough to understand that my father had passed away a few months before I was born. I grew up without him, and I can tell you it was not easy.

When I became of greater understanding, I came to find out that my father was killed during a fight when he was drunk. I also came to learn about the names and identities of the people who were involved in his death. Unfortunately, all of them were walking free in the village, and none of them was prosecuted. I came to hate those people with a very deep hatred. I made the choice that I will become a trial lawyer with the goal of fighting all the bad guys (including those men). My legal career of choice was a trial attorney. I wanted to be a trial attorney with the reputation of helping people to feel vindicated. Considering the kind of revenge and anger I had, I would have made a tough and mean-spirited criminal attorney. I would have become the type of attorney that is so aggressive that he makes sure every criminal rot in jail or rests in pieces. With the kind of anger and bitterness I had, I'm sure given a chance, the killers of my father would have had the ground literally shift from underneath their feet. I would have probably gone after their families and make them suffer until their heads begin spinning. Everything in me was crying for revenge. I was very driven and obsessed to get even. Sometimes the kind of vengeance I had felt like the collective anger of my family was resting on my shoulders. Looking back, I know I was beginning to turn into something that I would not have wished to become. What was growing in me was like the same stuff that monsters are made of.

In 1980 one of those men who was said to have delivered the fatal blow died after a long illness. As a 10-year-old boy, I went to the funeral, and I made sure he was dead and buried. It felt really good to see his body lowered into the grave. But that was just a temporary relief. I still felt that that was not enough. This was not just my pain alone. My family experienced a lot of pain and poverty because we had lost our main breadwinner. This was a huge blow that stayed with us every day. To some of us, it was unforgivable and unforgettable.

Everyone in my family was struggling with what to do. No matter how we looked at it, the experience of the loss of my father was a daily thing, and we could not find a way to shake it off.

Due to unforgiveness bitterness and pain of this loss, my family would not get along with all the people who were associated with that death. It also brought a wedge between the families. Some of the members of the family from my father's side were not in any talking terms with my side of the family. I grew up not knowing or acknowledging them as part of our family. I can remember as a kid walking to school with no shoes and with a half empty stomach and heart full of unresolved issues. One day I met with one of the people suspected of the death of my father. I refused to acknowledge their greetings or even recognize their presence. Everybody in the village knew that we don't speak to each other because they were suspect in the death of my father. After 15 years, some people came to try and resolve the issue. My family refused to let this matter be resolved. It was too painful, and the wounds were still fresh. Furthermore, we felt justified to be angry because we had not asked for this injustice they had brought upon us. A few years later we came to know the Lord and my whole family gave our life to Christ. The difficult thing is that even after we gave our life to Christ, we could not find the courage to allow forgiveness to happen. I believe a lot of people may be in a similar place. It is possible to know Jesus and still walk in unforgiveness.

As a born again believer, I struggled with this issue, and I kept on asking my family to begin the process of healing and reconciliation. Nothing came through. There was no success. Later on, I came to the United States and started a ministry. It was in the middle of one of my ministry experiences that the Lord laid on my heart to begin the process of healing and reconciliation of the family.

THE FORTY YEAR VISIT.

42 years after my father's death, I flew to Africa to go on a mission to initiate the process of reconciliation. I asked for permission from my mom to go in the name of the family and start the process. That permission was denied. I prayed about it, and I asked what I would do. I talked to some members of my family, and I asked them if they would accompany me to go and visit my other side of the family.

By that time, we had not gotten along for 42 years. The most valuable living link and patriarch of that other side of the family were now 90-years-old. He was homebound and blind. But the good news was that he was strong, energetic and with a very sharp memory. The following day I woke up early in the morning in fasting and prayer and drove straight to my father's side of the family. I had them open the gate to let me into their homestead. They had no idea who I was. I had one of my brothers accompany me. I went without making any announcement. I was fasting and praying under my breath believing God for a miracle of 42 years. By the time I arrived, my relatives who we had never spoken to, were just waking up from bed.

I was nervous, full of mixed emotions and completely aware of the magnitude of the moment at hand. Although the key person that I needed to deal with was very old and blind, I was able to introduce myself and build a rapport. It was so hard for him because he wanted so much to see how I looked like. But I described myself to him and allowed him to touch me and build his confidence that it was me and not someone else. We began with prayer and intercession. He called on the name of the Lord and thanked him for making that day to happen. Even before we spoke about the heavy matter that had brought us together, I could feel a great breakthrough as walls of division and bitterness were coming down. He told God to heal the divide and begin a new chapter of unity and reconciliation. Whenever you muster the courage to face your greatest fears, it will lose its power. Fear is nothing but False Evidence Appearing Real. It is a stronghold built on intimidation, guilt, shame, blame or other toxic emotions.

The room broke into a dead silence. It looked like we were both traveling. I was traveling back to 6 months before birth. On the other hand, my uncle was traveling back to over 90 years of his life. This time travel looked like over 100 years flashing before our eyes while yet time stood still. I knew we were in a kairos moment. This was a historical moment, and the annals of heaven were ready to record a turning point in our family.

I could not wait for the clock to turn backward. Finally, I sensed the moment was ripe. I went straight to the point. I have learned through experience how to go straight to the issue and face it headlong. I turned on my voice recorder on my phone and popped the first question. I wanted to know; who killed my father?

My uncle and I went through the history of the last 42 years. I was not interested in the details of that history. All that I wanted to know was the circumstances surrounding the death of my father. I believe I needed a closure. He went into details describing all of the things that happened before during and after the death of my father. I asked all kinds of questions that no one has ever been able to share with me. I learned the good the bad and the ugly of both my father and the family. It was not easy to hear the ugly side of my father. I always wanted to view him as a flawless victim of injustice. But I was struck by some of the things I heard. I learned about how he acted especially while under the influence of alcohol. I asked questions that I thought had no answer. This man although he was blind he had so much insight into the history and the circumstances surrounding the death of my father.

Although he may not have disclosed everything, he gave me enough information to help me find a closure. I came in with a very strong investigative mind. I grilled him on questions and issues that I am not able to disclose for now. I revisited all the legal investigations that were carried out at the time of the death. All fingers that pointed to certain people and how they used their position to scatter the evidence. We were both experiencing a beautiful catharsis moment.

Finally, I knew I had to focus on why I was there. I was not there to prove who is guilty and who is not. I was not there to find justice. I was not there to point fingers or prove anything. My assignment was to close the door of four decades of a dark family nightmare. We finally leaned on each other, began weeping even as we prayed. We wept some more, we hugged some more, and we blessed each other. We put to an end the longest family feud of my life. I could feel the strongholds of hatred, unforgiveness, and offenses literary coming down. This was a huge move of God considering that we had not seen anything like this in 42 years.

In front of me was a perfect opportunity to receive something more valuable than any money could buy. Here was my 90-year-old uncle, the only blood brother of my father. I remembered that even a father in a mess has a blessing in his mouth. I recognized the weight of the glory of this moment. It was like I saw through him the resemblance of my father that I never met. That's when I perceived that I'm in a prophetic moment. I had to honor him and allow him to bless me. That's when I asked him to release the father's blessing on me. He spoke that blessing, and I received it, and then I turned around and blessed him with a gift. This is the moment I was waiting for. The moment to find a closure and also to receive my father's blessing. God gave me more than I had asked. He opened a door of reconciliation not only for me but also for my entire family.

I was so excited because I recorded the whole moment on my phone. I had an audio-video and pictures of that experience. I could not wait to go to my mom and share this beautiful encounter I had on behalf of the family. I knew it was a shocker. Many of them were not as excited, but regardless, the job had already been done. God had closed a wound that had been opened for 42 years. Now that was the beginning of the healing of some very deep cuts and wounds.

It's very hard to forgive especially when the death of a loved one is involved. I understand how difficult it was for my mother to let go. But after getting the revelation of forgiveness, I understand there is no other choice but to forgive. That is why as an act of my will I took the initiative to cross the line and go to those who had offended my family and begin to see the healing take place.

A few years later, I went back to visit my uncle. We had a very good time together although he could not see me, I could tell his heart was so delighted and full to "see" me.

He asked me to make myself available to do his funeral and to take care of any issues in his family in case of his death. Today I am delighted to have been used by God to heal this wound that has been there for 42 years. To top it off, today my family has moved on. We still meet and mingle with members of families of those who killed my father. There's no bad blood anymore. It's a new day. I am blessed to say that I have nothing against any of the killers. God has brought healing and reconciliation.

You ask me how this feels. I'll tell you it feels like a thousand pounds of weight off my shoulders. Whew! What a feeling.

CHAPTER 2

THE STORY THAT INSPIRED MY FORGIVENESS.

Father forgive them for they do not know what
they are doing. Luke (Jesus Christ)

I recently met the producer/director of the movie, "End of the Spear". I had the opportunity to hear how much that movie has impacted countless of people around the world. For me, it was a natural inspiration because it mirrors most of my childhood experiences. My meeting and interaction with Dr. Kevin MacFee have been nothing but an awesome blessing.

Just for the right perspective, here is the story behind the movie "end of the spear."

In 1956, Steve was five years old when his father, Nate, flew a Piper Cruiser plane with four other missionaries into the jungles of Equador and dared to make contact with the most dangerous tribe known to man, the Waodani (whoa-DONNY) also known as "Auca," or naked savage.

After several months of exchanging gifts with the natives, the five men were speared multiple times and hacked to death with machetes.

One of the men in the tribe that fateful day was Mincaye (min-KY-yee). Years later Steve found out that Mincaye actually delivered the final spear that ultimately killed his father. (Three of the six warriors from that day are still alive.)

Today they consider themselves family and harbor no resentment. Steve says he has never forgotten the pain and heartache of losing his dad.

"But I can't imagine not loving Mincaye, a man who has adopted me as his own, and the other Waodani," says Steve, who made his first trip into Waodani territory when he was 9 years old.

By 1956 Steve's Aunt Rachel had been living in the jungle but not with the Waodani for several years. Rachel loved her younger brother (Steve's dad) like a son, but even after he was killed, she continued to live with the Waodani until her death in 1994. Her affection for them was a major influence in Steve's life. He visited her every summer.

When he was 14, Steve and his sister, Kathy, decided to be baptized and chose a couple of Waodani to perform the baptism in the same water next to the beach where their father was killed. After Rachel had died, the tribe asked Steve to live with them. (Steve and his family lived in the jungle for a year and a half.) "What the Waodani meant for evil, God used for good," says Steve. "Given the chance to rewrite the story, I would not be willing to change it."

Many are confounded by the relationship Steve has with Mincaye. He says that a *USAToday* reporter commented that if he were in Steve's shoes, he could "forgive Mincaye, maybe. But love him, that's morbid." Steve says that their relationship doesn't make sense unless you put God in the equation. Even though his dad's death was painful, Steve says Mincaye would not have adopted him, and he would not have been part of the mysterious, stoneage Waodani world. Also, thousands of people, who were stirred by the missionaries' deaths, would not have dedicated their lives to helping take the gospel to unreached groups like Waodani all over the world.

(Extract from CBN Website:

http://www1.cbn.com/end-spear-true-story)

CHAPTER 3

THE 33 PRINCIPLES TO INSPIRE YOUR FORGIVENESS

"Forgive up, forgave down, forgive all around."

1. Forgiveness realigns the posture of your heart before God.

"So Jesus answered and said to them, "Have faith in God. For assuredly, I say to you, whoever says to this mountain, 'Be removed and be cast into the sea,' and does not doubt in his heart, but believes that those things he says will be done, he will have whatever he says. Therefore I say to you, whatever things you ask when you pray, believe that you receive them, and you will have them. "And whenever you stand praying, if you have anything against anyone, forgive him, that your Father in heaven may also forgive you your trespasses. But if you do not forgive, neither will your Father in heaven forgive your trespasses."" Mark 11:22-26 NKJV

2. Forgiveness is one way to keep your heart pure and tender.

Eph 4:32, "Be kind to one another, tenderhearted, forgiving one another, as God in Christ forgave you."

3. Our walk with God is enhanced by the way we extend forgiveness to those who trespass us.

"But if you do not forgive others their trespasses, neither will your Father forgive your trespasses." Matt 6:14

4. Get it off your chest and lay it all before Him:

"If we confess our sins, He is faithful and just to forgive us our sins and to cleanse us from all unrighteousness." I John 1:9 NKJV

5. There's no unpardonable sin that we cannot forgive.

Then Peter came up and said to him, "Lord, how often will my brother sin against me, and I forgive him? As many as seven times?" Jesus said to him, "I do not say to you seven times, but seventy times seven. Matt 18:21-22

6. Forgiveness sets the atmosphere for healing to the deepest cuts and wounds.

"Therefore, confess your sins to one another and pray for one another, that you may be healed. The prayer of a righteous person has great power as it is effective". James 5:16

7. Leave no room for hate. Only love.

"But I say to you who hear, Love your enemies, do good to those who hate you"; Luke 6:27

8. The law of sowing and reaping works even in the realm of forgiveness. The more you give away, the more it comes back to you. Luke 6:37 "Forgive, and you will be forgiven";

9. Our degree of forgiveness is dependent on the depth of revelation we have about God's love and forgiveness to us.

"Bearing with one another and, if one has a complaint against another, forgiving each other; as the Lord has forgiven you, so you also must forgive." Col 3:13.

10. Forgiveness spells GRACE. It is an honor for God to allow us to show grace to others.

"He does not deal with us according to our sins, nor repay us according to our iniquities. For as high as the heavens are above the earth, so great is his steadfast love toward those who fear him; as far as the east is from the west, so far does he remove our transgressions from us. As a father shows compassion to his children, so the Lord shows compassion to those who fear him. For he knows our frame; he remembers that we are dust". Psalms 103:10-14

11. Nothing is too hard to forgive. God knows you can handle it. Just do it.

"No temptation has overtaken you that is not common to man. God is faithful, and he will not let you be tempted beyond your ability, but with the temptation, he will also provide the way of escape, that you may be able to endure it." 1 Cor 10:13

12. Hate does not live here. Only love.

"Hatred stirs up strife, but love covers all offenses." Prov 10:12

13. Nobody deserves forgiveness just in case you've forgotten.

"For all have sinned and fall short of the glory of God" Rom 3:23

14. I forgive because I'm grateful I have been forgiven:

Luke 7:44-50 "Therefore I tell you, her sins, which are many, are forgiven—for she loved much. But he who is forgiven little loves little." And he said to her, "Your sins are forgiven." ..

15. It's all about love love love. John 13:34

"A new commandment I give to you, that you love one another: just as I have loved you, you also are to love one another."

16. He forgave us so we can forgive. Matthew 6:12

"And forgive us our debts, as we also have forgiven our debtors."

17. Relationships thrive in the atmosphere of forgiveness.

"Whoever covers an offense seeks love, but he who repeats a matter separates close friends." Prov 17:9

18. Revival breaks out in an atmosphere of forgiveness.

"And Peter said to them, "Repent and be baptized every one of you in the name of Jesus Christ for the forgiveness of your sins, and you will receive the gift of the Holy Spirit." Acts 2:38

19. The finished work of Jesus on the cross paid the price to make it easy to receive and extend forgiveness. Matthew 26:28

"For this is my blood of the covenant, which is poured out for many for the forgiveness of sins."

20. Never withhold forgiveness regardless of how you feel;

"Pay attention to yourselves! If your brother sins, rebuke him, and if he repents, forgive him, and if he sins against you seven times in the day, and turns to you seven times, saying, 'I repent,' you must forgive him." Luke 17:3-4

21. God will never deny us forgiveness. Regardless of what you have done, always run to him and not away from him.

"If they sin against you—for there is no one who does not sin—and you are angry with them and give them to an enemy, so that they are carried away captive to the land of the enemy, far off or near, yet if they turn their heart in the land to which they have been carried captive, and repent and plead with you in the land of their captors, saying, 'We have sinned and have acted perversely and wickedly,' if they repent with all their mind and with all their heart in the land of their enemies, who carried them captive, and pray to you toward their land, which you gave to their fathers, the city that you have chosen, and the house that I have built for your name", 1 Kings 8:46-48

22. Forgive yourself. Break the root of condemnation.

"There is therefore now no condemnation for those who are in Christ Jesus." Rom 8:1

23. Be sincere in your prayer for forgiveness.

"Wash me thoroughly from my iniquity, and cleanse me from my sin! For I know my transgressions, and my sin is ever before me. Against you, you only, have I sinned and done what is evil in your sight, so that you may be justified in your words and blameless in your judgment. Behold, I was brought forth in iniquity, and in sin did my mother conceive me." Psalms 51:2-5

24. The royal law leads to loyal relationships.

"If you really fulfill the royal law according to the Scripture, "You shall love your neighbor as yourself," you are doing well. James 2:8

25. Make your forgiveness permanent and irreversible:

Jeremiah 31:34 "For I will forgive their iniquity, and I will remember their sin no more."

26. The atmosphere of forgiveness is the blooming ground for the fruit of the Spirit.

Galatians 5:22 "But the fruit of the Spirit is love, joy, peace, patience, kindness, goodness, faithfulness."

27. Jesus paid it all, so you don't have to bear it anymore.

"But he was wounded for our transgressions; he was crushed for our iniquities; upon him was the chastisement that brought us peace, and with his stripes, we are healed." Isaiah 53:5

28. Now is the time for a clean slate and a new beginning.

"Come now, let us reason together, says the Lord: though your sins are like scarlet, they shall be as white as snow; though they are red like crimson, they shall become like wool." Isaiah 1:18

29. God's nature in us empowers us to forgive.

"Who is a God like you, pardoning iniquity and passing over transgression for the remnant of his inheritance? He does not retain his anger forever because he delights in steadfast love. He will again have compassion on us; he will tread our iniquities underfoot. You will cast all our sins into the depths of the sea. You will show faithfulness to Jacob and steadfast love to Abraham, as you have sworn to our fathers from the days of old" Micah 7:18-20

30. Live by the Joseph principle.

What was meant for evil God will make it all good. You will enjoy a full life of blessings and great grace.

"When Joseph's brothers saw that their father was dead, they said, "Perhaps Joseph will hate us, and may actually repay us for all the evil which we did to him." So they sent messengers to Joseph, saying, "Before your father died he commanded, saying, 'Thus you shall say to Joseph: "I beg you, please forgive the trespass of your brothers and their sin; for they did evil to you." 'Now, please, forgive the trespass of the servants of the God of your father." And Joseph wept when they spoke to him. Then his brothers also went and fell down before his face, and they said, "Behold, we are your servants." Joseph said to them, "Do not be afraid, for am I in the place of God? But as for you, you meant evil against me; but God meant it for good, in order to bring it about as it is this day, to save many people alive. Now, therefore, do not be afraid; I will provide for you and your little ones." And he comforted them and spoke kindly to them. So Joseph dwelt in Egypt, he and his father's household. And Joseph lived one hundred and ten years. Joseph saw Ephraim's children to the third generation. The children of Machir, the son of Manasseh, were also brought up on Joseph's knees." Genesis 50:15-23 NKJV

31. Today is another person. Tomorrow may be you needing forgiveness

"Brethren, if a man is overtaken in any trespass, you who are spiritual restore such a one in a spirit of gentleness, considering yourself lest you also be tempted." Galatians 6:1 NKJV

32. Unforgiveness opens doors for demons to torment our lives. Shut the door and never open it again.

"Therefore the kingdom of heaven is like a certain king who wanted to settle accounts with his servants. And when he had begun to settle accounts, one was brought to him who owed him ten thousand talents. But as he was not able to pay, his master commanded that he be sold, with his wife and children and all that he had, and that payment be made. The servant, therefore, fell down before him, saying, 'Master, have patience with me, and I will pay you all.' Then the master of that servant was moved with compassion, released him, and forgave him the debt. "But that servant went out and found one of his fellow servants who owed him a hundred denarii; and he laid hands on him and took him by the throat, saying, 'Pay me what you owe!' So his fellow servant fell down at his feet and begged him, saying, 'Have patience with me, and I will pay you all.' And he would not, but went and threw him into prison till he should pay the debt. So when his fellow servants saw what had been done, they were very grieved, and came and told their master all that had been done. Then his master, after he had called him, said to him, 'You wicked servant! I forgave you all that debt because you begged me. Should you not also have had compassion on your fellow servant, just as I had pity on you?' And his master was angry and delivered him to the torturers until he should pay all that was due to him. "So My heavenly Father also will do to you if each of you, from his heart, does not forgive his brother his trespasses.'" Matthew 18:23-35 NKJV

CHAPTER 4

THE 7 LESSONS I LEARNT

"The most tragic story in life is the story of a man who chooses to learn nothing from their mistakes"
(Dr. Charles Karuku)

1. **When we don't forgive, the enemy has the upper hand in tormenting our lives.** Unforgiveness is one way that we open the door to be tormented by demons spirits. The Bible tells us of a story of a king who forgives the debt of one of his servants. Then that servant on his way home met a man who owed him very little. Immediately he forgot how much debt he had been forgiven. He began to harass the man who owed him very little. He beat him up, threw him into prison and demanded his debt to be paid immediately. Then the word got out to the king that the man he had forgiven has not forgiven another man that owned him a very little debt. The

king got angry and recalled the debt. He threw this wicked man into prison to be tormented by demons. Sometimes the torment of fear, insecurity, jealousy, bitterness, anger, anxiety, depression, resentment, and all kinds of torments could be rooted in unforgiveness.

This is the time to close the door on unforgiveness. Most people will find more peace and closure after forgiveness. All of the torment of sleeplessness and depression can be wiped away by the simple act of forgiveness.

2. **I learned about healing in forgiveness.** There is something called forgiveness therapy. This type of therapy acknowledges that there is a direct connection between sickness and disease with unforgiveness. Statistics have proven that there are people suffering from incurable diseases that are rooted in unforgiveness. The Bible says that unforgiveness dries up the bones. It is a known fact that arthritis can be rooted in unforgiveness. It is also a scientific fact that unforgiveness raises the level of stress that is likely to complicate the process of healing. Breast cancer has been linked to unforgiveness. Most women surveyed who have had breast cancer have been seen to have anger issues with another woman. Irritability, migraines, high blood pressure, heart attacks and stomach ulcers

have been linked to stress. It is a known fact that anger coming from unforgiveness can escalate stress levels and trigger shock, heart attack, high blood pressure, stroke, muscle tensions, ulcers, and migraines.

Of course, we know unforgiveness is a sin. We also know that sickness and disease came into the world through the door of the sin of Adam and Eve. Today I believe many people will experience supernatural healing as a result of forgiveness.

Since God called me into ministry in 1991, I have seen the lame walk, the blind see, the deaf hear, tumors disappear and many diseases healed. There have been times when the Holy Spirit has spoken to me to have people repent and forgive to experience healing. I pray that many here today are going to experience the healing of deep cuts and wounds. Many new chapters are going to be opened. The key is forgiveness.

3. When we forgive God forgives us too.

Matt 6:14-15

"For if ye forgive men their trespasses, your heavenly Father will also forgive you: But if ye forgive not men their trespasses, neither will your Father forgive your trespasses."

4. **It makes you feel good and free from the poison of toxic emotions: lightness, light-hearted, joy and peace. Oh, what a relief!**

PEACE: It is a tranquility where there is nothing broken and nothing missing in your life. It is well with you. It is well with your relationship with God and with others. That's the fullness and sweetness of the Shalom peace of God.

5. **God accepts your offerings as true offerings when you forgive.** Unforgiveness defiles or contaminates your service to God.

"Therefore if you bring your gift to the altar, and there remember that your brother has something against you, leave your gift there before the altar, and go your way. First, be reconciled to your brother, and then come and offer your gift." Matthew 5:23-24 NKJV

6. **Prayers are heard when you forgive.** I found there's a better quality of life after forgiveness.

1 Peter 3:7-"Likewise, ye husbands, dwell with them according to knowledge, giving honor unto the wife, as unto the weaker vessel, and as being heirs together of the grace of life; that your prayers be not hindered."

7. **It is a sign of spiritual maturity.** It reveals that we have received an understanding of what Christ has done for us and we are able to extend it to others.

"Love endures long and is patient and kind; love never is envious nor boils over with jealousy, is not boastful or vainglorious, does not display itself haughtily. It is not conceited (arrogant and inflated with pride); it is not rude (unmannerly) and does not act unbecomingly. Love (God's love in us) does not insist on its own rights or its own way, for it is not self-seeking; it is not touchy or fretful or resentful; it takes no account of the evil done to it [it pays no attention to a suffered wrong]. It does not rejoice at injustice and unrighteousness but rejoices when right and truth prevail. Love bears up under anything and everything that comes is ever ready to believe the best of every person, its hopes are fadeless under all circumstances, and it endures everything [without weakening]. Love never fails [never fades out or becomes obsolete or comes to an end]. 1 Corinthians 13:4-8 AMP

CHAPTER 5

UNDERSTANDING FORGIVENESS THERAPY. HOW UNFORGIVENESS AFFECTS YOUR HEALTH

"It is hard to forgive when you feel justified to be angry."

SCRIPTURES AND SCIENCE AGREE ON THIS.

Prov 17:22-a Merry heart is a good medicine, but a crushed or bitter spirit dries up the bones.

Saul's jealousy and resentment for the success of David was the cause of his depression. The tormenting spirits gave him feats of depression which came with anger and violence.

"But the Spirit of the LORD departed from Saul, and a distressing spirit from the LORD troubled him. And Saul's servants said to him, "Surely, a distressing spirit from God is troubling you. Let our master now command your servants, who are before you, to seek out a man who is a skillful player on the harp. And it shall be that he will play it with his hand when the distressing spirit from God is upon you, and you shall be well." So Saul said to his servants, "Provide me now a man who can play well, and bring him to me." Then one of the servants answered and said, "Look, I have seen a son of Jesse the Bethle-hemite, who is skillful in playing, a mighty man of valor, a man of war, prudent in speech, and a handsome person; and the LORD is with him."

And so it was, whenever the spirit from God was upon Saul, that David would take a harp and play it with his hand. Then Saul would become refreshed and well, and the distressing spirit would depart from him."

I Samuel 16:14-18, 23 NKJV

Apostle John writing to Gais recognized the connection between physical health and emotional health. He says in 3 John 2, "Beloved, I pray that you may prosper in all things and be in health, just as your soul prospers." The health and wellness of the body prosper at the degree of the health and wellbeing of the soul (which includes the mind and emotions).

When we refuse to forgive, there's a possibility that such an act will increase stress levels in the body by up to 90%. Such a heightened surge in stress levels can result in making anything wrong with your body become worse. It can also deplete the immune system and make the body vulnerable to all kinds of attacks by sickness and diseases. This worsening state of the body may become a factor in determining how well the body heals itself or how good it responds to medical treatment. That being said, the opposite is true. Forgiveness lowers the stress levels, boosts your chances of keeping the body functional and capable of fighting sicknesses and diseases.

What are some of the most significant health problems related to stress? Here's a sampling.

I found this article very interesting. I think it explains in the most basic terms the importance of the connection between emotional and physical health.

Heart disease. Researchers have long suspected that the Stressed-out, type A personality has a higher risk of high blood pressure and heart problems. We don't know why, exactly. Stress can directly increase heart rate and blood flow and causes the release of cholesterol and triglycerides into the blood stream. It's also possible that stress is related to other problems -- an increased likelihood of smoking or obesity -- that indirectly increase the heart risks. Doctors do know that sudden emotional stress can be a trigger for serious cardiac problems, including heart attacks. People who have chronic heart problems need to avoid acute stress -- and learn how to successfully manage life's unavoidable stresses -- as much as they can.

Asthma. Many studies have shown that stress can worsen asthma. Some evidence suggests that a parent's chronic stress might even increase the risk of developing asthma in their children. One study looked at how parental stress affected the asthma rates of young children who were also exposed to air pollution or whose mothers smoked during pregnancy. The kids with stressed out parents had a substantially higher risk of developing asthma.

Obesity. Excess fat in the belly seems to pose greater health risks than fat on the legs or hips -- and unfortunately, that's just where people with high stress seem to store it. "Stress causes higher levels of the hormone cortisol," says Winner, "and that seems to increase the amount of fat that's deposited in the abdomen."

Diabetes. Stress can worsen diabetes in two ways. First, it increases the likelihood of bad behaviors, such as unhealthy eating and excessive drinking. Second, stress seems to raise the glucose levels of people with type 2 diabetes directly.

Headaches. Stress is considered one of the most common triggers for headaches -- not just tension headaches, but migraines as well.

Depression and anxiety. It's probably no surprise that chronic stress is connected with higher rates of depression and anxiety. One survey of recent studies found that people who had stress related to their jobs -- like demanding work with few rewards -- had an 80% higher risk of developing depression within a few years than people with lower stress.

Gastrointestinal problems. Here's one thing that stress doesn't do -- it doesn't cause ulcers. However, it can make them worse. Stress is also a common factor in many other GI conditions, such as chronic heartburn (or gastroesophageal reflux disease, GERD) and irritable bowel syndrome (IBS), Winner says.

Alzheimer's disease. One animal study found that stress might worsen Alzheimer's disease, causing its brain lesions to form more quickly. Some researchers speculate that reducing stress has the potential to slow down the progression of the disease.

Accelerated aging. There's actually evidence that stress can affect how you age. One study compared the DNA of mothers who were under high stress -- they were caring for a chronically ill child -- with women who were not. Researchers found that a particular region of the chromosomes showed the effects of accelerated aging. Stress seemed to accelerate aging about 9 to 17 additional years.

Premature death. A study looked at the health effects of stress by studying elderly caregivers looking after their spouses -- people who are naturally under a great deal of stress. It found that caregivers had a 63% the higher rate of death than people their age who were not caregivers.

(Article on Web MD by R. Morgan Griffin; http://www.webmd.com/balance/stress-management/features/10-fixable-stress-related-health-problems#1)

PROFILES OF FORGIVENESS

Here are some stories from some of my students who have practiced forgiveness therapy while battling sickness and diseases. Most of my students have now become experts on this subject. I hope their story helps you in your journey as well.

HEALING TESTIMONY FROM LIZ

Some years ago, I received this testimony from Liz. She is not only a great student but also a practitioner of the forgiveness therapy. I'm so grateful for the understanding Liz has on this subject.

Liz had a huge decision she was trying to make at a critical stage of her life. But she needed the approval of both parents, particularly her mother. After many times of being denied, she decided to try one more time. On that particular night, she went over for dinner hoping to smoothen things up. Sometimes we can get a lot done over a meal. But this time, the meal was not doing the trick. When she went to her parent's house, the tension in the room was palpable. The atmosphere was unusually awkward and hard to read. The food was hot and delicious. The smell filled the room. But the stench of the tension drowned the beauty of the setting. Nobody seemed to have an appetite. Finally, Liz and her family sat down for dinner. As the food was being served and they were ready to begin talking, there was very little they could do to make things work out smoothly. It looked like both Liz and her mom were at the extreme ends of the spectrum and no hope for a happy medium. Everyone was stuck on their right to be heard and be right.

Finally, they realized that the conversation was not going anywhere. Instead of it going smoothly, it was going from bad to worse. It became hard to stop the escalation. To avoid making it a shouting match, Liz decided to remove herself from the situation and head back to her apartment. As Liz stood up to walk away to her car, her mother shouted to her and made this penetrating statement; "What you're doing is unforgivable, unforgivable, unforgivable," she said. Those words shot like a dart of fire through the ears and soul of Liz. But they kept going further and deeper into her body. She felt tension and stiffening. It was getting more and more into the hands and particularly the wrists. It did not feel normal. The tense and stiff feeling began migrating further and deeper into her wrists. It was taking over like a plague from a spell like the type we see in a horror movie.

Words have power. These words, coming from an authority figure, were also loaded with anger and pain of heart. That is why as soon as the words left the mouth of her mother, Liz began to experience a very weird reaction. Immediately her wrists began to stiffen up in a way that was similar to the beginning stages of arthritis. The stiffness began getting stronger and harder. The wrists began to tighten more and more. It was very scary for Liz to watch her wrists begin to twist right before her eyes. Suddenly, things began making sense for Liz. Just as the Bible teaches that bitterness dries up the bones, the spirit of bitterness in her had begun to work against her. She began to examine her own life. She realized how vulnerable she made herself by opening the door of bitterness and unforgiveness. She began to repent and ask God for forgiveness. She forgave her mother and began speaking blessings over their life and family. She spoke life to their relationship.

Doing the forgiveness thing was not easy for Liz. However, the thought of not doing it meant having to deal with unbearable consequences of arthritis. This whole process took three days. It involved a daily prayer of forgiveness and Liz speaking life to her relationship with the mother. After closing the door of unforgiveness, Liz commanded the stiffness of the wrists to go in Jesus name. Immediately, it left and has never returned. By the time of the writing of this book, Liz is still walking in the fullness of health and her relationship with her mom has been restored. Praise God.

HOW I WALKED A COUPLE THROUGH FORGIVENESS AFTER AN AFFAIR.

One of the hardest things I have ever witnessed again and again is a couple coming to me with so much mixed emotions due to an affair. As my wife likes to call it, it's the ultimate betrayal. Trust, fidelity and a sense of giving yourself away is the essence of what builds a strong marriage.

An affair is a dark stain that may be the hardest to fully erase from the marriage dress. It is a stain-filled with guilt, shame, self-blame, rejection, resentment, and worthlessness. It is a stain that has the ability to bleach trust. It is a sore stain that inflicts pain during the most intimate moments and causes the person to freeze and shut down sexually and emotionally. It has the potential of tainting the filters through which a person sees their spouse. If not properly removed, there may not be any hope for the marriage.

Over and over again, this breach of trust creates emotions that the other spouse has no ability to help heal or comfort. In a movie where a husband is cheating on his wife, it's common to hear women in the movie theater glitch and seethe with anger when they watch the cheating scene. But when it is exposed, and the woman gets vindicated, you can almost hear the sigh of relief and joy when justice is served. People who have gone through affairs have lived to tell us that they would not wish it on their worst enemy.

There's no formula for doing it right. The process of navigating through an affair is murky and painful at the same time. It requires velvet gloves and tough love applied at right times and in right measures. It requires applying the same measure of grace you would like to have extended to you if you were to be in such a situation. The toughest thing is to be the counselor. It requires the ability to walk on the tightrope of having to play this role without feelings of self-righteousness.

I will combine different experiences and of course not mention any names. I have helped several couples in this situation. Some of them had been through the experience years before. The others were fresh in it.

I'll tell you a story of a couple where the one who had an affair was unwilling to show up. But the one cheated on came to me and poured out their wretched heart. My wife and I sat there taking it all in and boy was it a hard pill to take! Such a story affects women more than men in many situations. Adultery is not just a sin of betrayal. It is also a thing of feeling rejected, unwanted, not good enough and not able to give what your cheating partner is looking for. I found the women who came to me asking questions which only women can ask. How tall was she? Was she younger? And was she thinner? What color of the hair was she? Was the hair blonde, black or what? Was she black? White? Spanish? Asian? or other? What made you attracted to her and not me?

Such questions come out of the insecurities that all women have. Many women don't feel beautiful enough. An affair is one way to embolden that feeling and legitimize it. It is just another crushing blow to an already insecure person.

My first step has always been to sit there, listen and let the person vent and cry. Without saying a word, I want to give them time to get it all out and lay it all out. I was helping this couple where the husband had cheated with another younger woman who in appearance looked more attractive than his wife. This put the woman in a very awkward position. She overreacted to get her husband back. She was unwilling to let a seductive woman steal her man. In a reaction to retake her stuff and protect the territory, she chose to do a quick reconciliation to get her man back. Although ultimately this is the right decision, it wasn't done with the right motives and after the right process. Needless to say, as soon as the husband went back home, the bitterness of the affair resurfaced and ultimately destroyed the marriage. She ended up losing him after all. Some people forgive, but they don't heal properly. I was so heartbroken that we could not save this marriage.

In my counseling sessions, I take the cheater and the cheated as two people that deserve to be treated with honor and respect. Although we all hate the sin of betrayal, we should always love and treat the sinner with dignity. Bringing honor and dignity into the process of counseling sets the right atmosphere for healing to begin. Sometimes the cheater is presented as a devil, and the cheated is elevated into a status of a saint. The truth is, there are reasons why people get into affairs. Although nothing should justify it, some have been pushed to the tipping point by the way they are mishandled in their marriages. In most of the cheating spouses I have spoken to, so many common factors are cited. Lack of affection, a dead marriage, rejection, abuse and more. But of course, for some, it is simply who they are. There are some spouses who are so starved of love, affection, sex or romance and they will be totally swept off their feet if they get any attention from someone out there. I like to consider there are factors that led to it. However, regardless of what the factors are, it is vital to take a position of zero tolerance of affairs. The commitment to fidelity is a cardinal value that is at the bedrock of a strong marriage.

As a counselor willing to mitigate the process of rebuilding trust, I have to establish the thinking behind the affair. I recognize this is the way we get a closure as humans. We don't want to dwell, at the point of shifting blame and making one person feel like they are worthless. My goal is to lead this process to become a win-win for all the people involved.

For another couple I worked with, it was a very different journey. They were married for many years and with children. Their marriage had hit a very tough spot. Needless to say, there were a lot of fights and broken communication.

The woman never felt affection, and the man did not feel appreciated or respected at home. Both tended to gravitate to their workplace where the man was well respected and admired. The workplace for the woman made her feel loved and seen as beautiful. Needless to say, they turned their home into a hotbed of conflict and chaos. As they say, the grass is always greener in the neighbor's yard. This situation as it continued added more pressure to the man. It magnified his weaknesses and put him in a vulnerable situation.

There was this attractive woman at work that made him feel so loved and admired. Like a perfect storm, everything was lining up slowly and making calculated steps to seduce and steal his heart away. This woman slowly began to become awfully close and open to flirting with him. She kept on making those signals and leaving impressions that stuck with him. She got him thinking, imagining and wondering how life would look like if things would suddenly shift and get them together. Little did he realize how this woman was slowly capturing his imagination and meeting some deep emotional needs. Slowly it kept on going, and finally, it crossed the line.

I found myself listening, comforting, loving and helping to hold their hands through the journey. Our first sessions were full of raw emotions. There was a lot of crying, regrets, shame, guilt, blame, finger pointing and so many mixed emotions that made it so hard to say one thing or the other. I spent most of those sessions listening. I made it a biweekly thing and then weekly. I tried to be there to support and listen and not judge. I encouraged them to do everything possible to move their marriage in the direction of healing, repentance, forgiveness and restoration.

We all agreed that it was the best thing to do. We made a choice to avoid anything that would sabotage our healing progress. It wasn't easy. Some days were worse than others. Other days it was one step forward and one step backward. Other days it felt like three steps forward and two backward. The thing that kept us going was we were committed to plow through it and see what is at the end.

The couple reaffirmed their love for each other. They did most of the heavy lifting on their own. There were long nights and hard days. But they seemed to be aware that for them to move forward, they will need a roadmap.

I provided the following roadmap. I like keeping it very simple. The first act of business was to cut off the relationship with the other woman. I made it mandatory for the man to terminate all contact and reconnect with the wife. I highly recommend one to remove themselves completely from the presence of the person they had an affair with. This is a non-negotiable concession that must be put in place in order to make meaningful progress. Without it, the rest of the effort will be as futile as trying to push air balloons into water.

Then we began the long process of rebuilding trust. It started with a simple commitment. I needed it to move on. The commitment was for the cheater to be given permission to earn the trust again. It's what I call total disclosure. It included opening up and being accountable about all the communication platforms and interactions that are going on every day through all channels including a phone call, phone logins, texts, email and social media. We were able to put those firm structures in place and then build a follow-up plan for marriage maintenance. This program to help the marriage rebuild and stay healthy. I had to convince the husband that trust must be earned. It may mean giving up some rights and privileges in exchange to earning trust.

We did everything to give the wife a sense of security in those measures that were put in place to rebuild trust. That was one guiding principle that enabled the wife to put a tracking device on the husband's phone. Also, she required him to call every time he would meet anyone in any other location away from work. He was simply trying to show accountability of his time and movements. Sometimes we have to do what we have to do to rebuild trust. Helping people after infidelity could be hard. But it is worth the effort when you finally get the marriage saved and family restored!

HOW I FORGAVE MYSELF

When I was a young boy in elementary school, I got exposed to pornography. I did not have any clue what it was. As a kid, this was like being introduced to drugs. I did not know what kind of a world of horror my little mind was getting to. It quickly became like a bottomless pit of fantasy. Nothing looked thrilling enough. Deeper and deeper, the pit went. Darker and darker, the pit became and so did my life. My curious mind got wrapped up in the web of the world that began to become so hard and almost impossible to untangle. Growing up with those images of a world of fantasy embedded in my mind was like having a tumor stuck in the brain and sending grotesque images into all areas of my life. When I became born again, it did not stop. I found myself in college and still struggling with the urges for pornography.

Somehow, I went through my first years of college life carrying a lot of guilt, shame and bearing a deep root of condemnation. The more I grew up and had more self-awareness, the more I did not like myself. I was filled with a lot of self-hatred, shame, and condemnation. I did not have a very good body image or self-esteem. I hated myself and even my life as a whole. People would see me and probably want to be me. But little did they know how much I hated myself.

One day in a very huge moment of failure and disappointment with my life, things began crumbling around me. I felt like a failure. I had no hope. I was angry with myself and just wanted to die. The problem was that I did not know how to commit suicide. I feared that if I kill myself, I'll end up in hell. During that time, I was naive enough to ask God to assist me in committing suicide. I prayed a simple prayer, "God, please kill me." It is true God answers prayers. And the most powerful prayers are the most simple ones. He answered my prayers but not the way I thought. I had a very tremendous and firm voice that spoke to me in the inside with these words, "Charles, it's not you that needs to die, but something in you needs to die." And that was what I truly needed. Something in me? What is that something? That's when I started a soul searching. At the core of my being was the old man. As a child, struggling with pornography and being a grown up adult, I had shamed myself. I hated myself. A shame-based identity had become my identity. My old nature was still alive and well in me. I carried a deep sense of guilt, shame, condemnation and self-hatred. Every time I did something wrong, instead of having Godly sorrow that leads to repentance and acceptance, the opposite happened. I dived into condemnation and total hopelessness. When I failed, my identity would become the identity of a failure. I saw no hope for redemption and suicide was the only option. Instead of facing my fears, I opted for suicide, which is simply, a permanent solution for a temporary situation. God had finally given me my key to my freedom.

He began to teach me how to forgive and love myself. I realized you cannot love others on empty. You must first love yourself, and then you can overflow with love for others. That was the beginning of a journey to love myself. Growing up, people would say, "shame on you" as a way to shame me. Words have power. I recognized how powerful those words were. They seemed to speak shame to me and became the foundation of a shame-based identity. Eventually, every time I failed and slipped into anything like pornography, I quickly went into a mode of shame. I had to begin speaking to myself over and over that I will never be ashamed. Jesus bore my shame. I had to learn how not to carry shame. By learning to despise the shame by focusing on the good in my life, I finally broke the back of a shame-based identity.

Not very long ago, I had a situation where someone came to confront me on something that I had done. I had done something that was not uplifting to them. I was truly wrong and sincerely wrong. When I look back, I see how God has helped me to overcome a shame-based identity. This person brought another friend with them to put me under the carpet. Their intention was to shame me. They laid out their case, and I quickly admitted my wrong and asked for their forgiveness. However, one of them hesitated to grant forgiveness because they thought I was not ashamed enough and falling on my face in tears about it. I had simply refused to accept a shame-based identity. Shame is not part of our inheritance or identity. It is a yoke of bondage. I refuse to take shame when the word of God tells me that Jesus took my shame. I simply repented and refused to embrace shame. Instead, I embraced conviction and Godly sorrow that leads to repentance. Finally, I can say my shame is gone. I have been set free. O what a freedom!

Now I love myself. I love my body image. I have accepted myself the way God created me. I'm no longer a slave of shame. I am free. When we forgive ourselves, we become best friends with ourselves. We also overcome the stronghold of guilt, shame, blame, and the root of condemnation. Do not allow yourself to be defined by shame. Begin today to forgive yourself. One of the ways I did it was to say I am loved, I am accepted, and I am highly favored of the Lord. I'm not ashamed. The greater one lives inside of me. He bore my shame. He was chastised for me. I can rest in his victory. His name is Jesus.

FORGIVING A FATHER OR A MOTHER.

It is called the father's wound. It is the anger that many people carry towards their father of mother. The book of Malachi closes the Old Testament with a very powerful statement worth of our attention. It's a prophetic word that speaks to our generation;

"Behold, I will send you Elijah the prophet Before the coming of the great and dreadful day of the LORD. And he will turn The hearts of the fathers to the children, And the hearts of the children to their fathers, Lest I come and strike the earth with a curse.'" Malachi 4:5-6 NKJV

This verse is also a warning that lives out among us every day everywhere. When the heart of the father is not turned to the children, and when the heart of the children has turned away from the fathers, the earth is struck with a curse. What kind of a curse? It's what I call the curse of a fatherless generation. It's a bunch of angry people who suffer from a father fracture that has never healed. It's the generational curse of a people rejected, abandoned and mishandled by a father who was not fully present in the life of their children.

The father's wound manifests in the following ways;

1. **Bastards:** This is an unruly, undisciplined child who has been born outside the covenant of marriage. A bastard lacks the love of the father. They feel like they are a mistake. They feel like a product of lust and not love. There's a possibility of rejection from the womb. Other bastards have survived abortion. When fathers refuse to acknowledge or be present in the lives of their children, they may cause them to become or feel like bastards. Paul warns that if we do

not discipline our children, they will become bastards. Part of the discipline is discipleship. It is the training and the leadership we offer to them that makes them confident to become better fathers. Bastards breed bastards. It's a generational curse that will keep self-propagating unless it is broken from spreading.

God is a lover of bastards. Regardless of the circumstances that surround our birth, God planned and purposed for us to be born. It doesn't matter how we came. It doesn't even matter whether we were born out of rape, prostitution or a one night stand. No one ever comes to the world without God allowing it. Even before we got into the mother's womb, God knew us and ordained our birth. I break the curse of the bastard in Jesus name. You're loved and accepted.

2. **Vagabonds:** these are wanderers like Cain. He was the first vagabond. He became so because of his refusal to repent after killing his brother. There are sons who have sinned against their fathers. They have refused to repent and are being haunted by their sin. They are operating under a curse. They are also on the run. One of the characteristics of a vagabond is that they are nomadic and do not settle down. They are not connected well to people around them. They are also not planted. As a result, they do not grow deep roots neither are they able to grow into maturity

and bear fruits. Lack of stability is their undoing. Most of them break their marriages, do not keep jobs and are unable to be established well in life. They lack what it takes to have the stability that causes one to break ground and thrive.

Being a vagabond is healed by humility and then repenting of the sins and accepting love. God is a father to the vagabonds. He has a big heart and wants them to settle down and simply sit at his feet and accept his love. Vagabonds must find a person they trust and allow themselves to be planted and grounded.

3. **Orphans:** These are those that are angry for reasons beyond their control. They are those who have lost their father through death, divorce or abandonment. That used to be me. Orphans are angry, grieving and sad. They are also a little more traumatized than the other categories of wounded sons. Orphans ask the question, "why me?". They are constantly sad and feeling very insecure. Their struggle is real. They do not feel confident to step into their place. Jesus promised us that we shall not be left comfortless like orphans. He promised to send us the Holy Spirit to be our comforter, teacher, and companion. The power of the Holy Spirit is the greatest healing for orphans. No amount of proving themselves can truly comfort like God.

4. **Prodigals:** This category of sons could even be from a very stable and loving home. The prodigal son in Luke 15 had a very loving and wealthy father. The reason they became a prodigal was a matter of their choice and wanting to rebel. They were simply trying something else other than the love of their father's house. They wanted to go to the big city and experience wild living. Sometimes we opt to rebel against God for our own reasons. The prodigals sometimes get out of their senses, and they practice nonsensical behaviors. But when the prodigal son hit the rock bottom of his rebellious choices, he came back to himself and decided to arise and go back to his father in repentance. Prodigals need to be loved unconditionally just like other wayward sons. A father of the prodigal is always the standard bearer of fatherhood after all. When the prodigal searches other lovers and places, they will finally hit the rock bottom and realize there's no other loving father like their father. They will finally repent and return. The question is, will the father recognize the return of their son and receive them without overreacting and wounding them?

It's the tragedy of a fatherless generation that produces orphans, prodigals, bastards and vagabonds. While orphans are sad and feel abandoned, prodigals are rebellious and on the run wasting away their potential. They are wild and careless. They are fueled by filth and fury of a father's fracture. The bastards feel rejected by fathers who have denied them of affection, affirmation, allowance and attention. On the other hand, vagabonds are unstable and nomadic due to restlessness. They lack the ability to stay committed and follow through. Due to an endless cycle of broken focus, vagabonds are unable to grow deep roots that would enable them to thrive into credible levels of maturity.

A lot of studies have been carried out on the subject of the father's wound. It is common knowledge that most of the criminals, school dropouts, divorcees, jobless people and all categories of failure in life, have one common denominator. Most of them carry a father's wound. A survey of prostitutes, abused people, abusers, suicide victims, world dictators and drug addicts also reveal the common trait of a father's wound. What makes this the case? The Bible command us to honor the father and the mother and attaches this commandment with a promise. The honor of parents leads to long life and things being well (prosperity) in earthly life. We must not allow our anger towards our parents to lead to dishonor. I always say that whenever there's an issue between a parent and a child, regardless of who is on the wrong side, it is the child that carries the greatest amount of consequences.

In the process of forgiving the parents, we must allow the heart to shift towards them in love. True forgiveness not only has a heart realignment but also it is a heart thing. That is why without touching the heart, nothing else can offer full complete transformation. Choose to forgive from the heart. Let the grudges go. One of the ways I have successfully forgiven my parents and also helped people to forgive is by counting the positives of what your parents mean to you. Celebrate them for the fact that they gave birth to you, took good care of you when you were yet helpless and raised you to be who you're today. Also, focus on the plan of God who chose them to birth you and not other random persons. Recognize and respect the original intention of God to use those parents to bring you into the world. Forget and overlook all the other circumstances. Only consider the plan of God. As you allow those words and thoughts to run through your spirit, you will begin to overflow with love and affection for your parents.

Also, find a way to honor your parents in the best way possible. Do it while they're still alive. When your parents speak well of you, it is a blessing. Make peace with your parents now and not later.

The issue of the father's wound is the cause of most of the dysfunctions we have in our nation. As the father goes, so goes the family. As the family goes, so goes the community. As the community goes, so goes the nation. Only forgiveness will heal our land from this curse that is like a plague spreading in our generation.

Here are some very damning statistics.

- 63% of youth suicides are from fatherless homes (US Dept. Of Health/Census) – 5 times the average.
- 90% of all homeless and runaway children are from fatherless homes – 32 times the average.
- 85% of all children who show behavior disorders come from fatherless homes – 20 times the average. (Center for Disease Control)
- 80% of rapists with anger problems come from fatherless homes –14 times the average. (Justice & Behavior, Vol 14, p. 403-26)
- 71% of all high school dropouts come from fatherless homes – 9 times the average. (National Principals Association Report)

Father Factor in Education – Fatherless children are twice as likely to drop out of school.

- Children with Fathers who are involved are 40% less likely to repeat a grade in school.
- Children with Fathers who are involved are 70% less likely to drop out of school.
- Children with Fathers who are involved are more likely to get A's in school.

- Children with Fathers who are involved are more likely to enjoy school and engage in extracurricular activities.
- 75% of all adolescent patients in chemical abuse centers come from fatherless homes – 10 times the average.

Father Factor in Drug and Alcohol Abuse – Researchers at Columbia University found that children living in two-parent household with a poor relationship with their father are 68% more likely to smoke, drink, or use drugs compared to all teens in two-parent households. Teens in single mother households are at a 30% higher risk than those in two-parent households.

- 70% of youths in state-operated institutions come from fatherless homes – 9 times the average. (U.S. Dept. of Justice, Sept. 1988)
- 85% of all youths in prison come from fatherless homes – 20 times the average. (Fulton Co. Georgia, Texas Dept. of Correction)

Father Factor in Incarceration – Even after controlling for income, youths in father-absent households still had significantly higher odds of incarceration than those in mother-father families. Youths who never had a father in the household experienced the highest odds. A 2002 Department of Justice survey of 7,000 inmates revealed that 39% of jail inmates lived in mother-only households. Approximately forty-six percent of jail inmates in 2002 had a previously incarcerated family member. One-fifth experienced a father in prison or jail.

Father Factor in Crime – A study of 109 juvenile offenders indicated that family structure significantly predicts delinquency. Adolescents, particularly boys, in single-parent families were at higher risk of status, property and person delinquencies. Moreover, students attending schools with a high proportion of children of single parents are also at risk. A study of 13,986 women in prison showed that more than half grew up without their father. Forty-two percent grew up in a single-mother household, and sixteen percent lived with neither parent

Father Factor in Child Abuse – Compared to living with both parents, living in a single-parent home doubles the risk that a child will suffer physical, emotional, or educational neglect. The overall rate of child abuse and neglect in single-parent households is 27.3 children per 1,000, whereas the rate of overall maltreatment in two-parent households is 15.5 per 1,000.

Daughters of single parents without a Father involved are 53% more likely to marry as teenagers, 711% more likely to have children as teenagers, 164% more likely to have a pre-marital birth and 92% more likely to get divorced themselves.

Adolescent girls raised in a 2 parent home with involved Fathers are significantly less likely to be sexually active than girls raised without involved Fathers.

https://thefatherlessgeneration.wordpress.com/statistics/

I don't expect prisons to reform these persons. The root of their crime is deeper that meets the eye. It is time to allow forgiveness therapy into our correctional institutions. At the heart of their reformation is the matters of their heart.

FORGIVENESS AFTER AN ABORTION

Abortion is America's Holocaust that is silently happening every day. The scourge of abortion has turned into a genocide in grand scale. By the time of writing this book, we have had over 50 million abortions globally. Just imagine, one baby is aborted every 26 seconds. As you're busy reading this book, the blood of innocent children is running under the drainages of our cities and nations. As we are going on with our daily lives, the blood of these innocent angels cries from underneath our feet, but we are probably too busy to notice.

What you probably don't know is that the innocent babies slaughtered through partial birth abortion and other brutal procedures may be dead and silenced. But the men and women behind these acts are still walking around haunted by the memories of their choices. Most of those people do not know where to go for healing. Some of them struggle with guilt, shame, self-blame, condemnation, fear, and anxiety. There are others who are dealing with depression. The spiritual consequences of abortion are much more devastating than any other loss of a loved one. It is a death of a baby without a funeral and no closure. It is the death of a baby that one would have loved to death if they ever had a chance to hold it. Abortion is the death of a baby that one chose over a life of comfort and convenience. Abortion is the death of a baby that was self-instigated and done in secret. It's a secret sin that haunts someone in secrecy for the rest of their life unless they find a way to get freedom.

Abortion falls under the category of shedding innocent blood. Every time innocent blood is shed, it opens wounds in the earth that cry out to heaven. The blood of Abel, shed by Cain began crying out to God for revenge. Every time innocent blood begins to cry out, it opens a legal ground for the enemy to wage a battle in the mind and lay all kinds of accusations against someone. I have dealt with people who have had multiple issues coming through the sin of abortion. We had a situation of someone who had issues with female organs, and the Lord revealed it was from abortion. Some people have used abortion as a form of birth control. Only God knows how many babies they have aborted! There's in many situations a strong connection between sexual sin and abortion. Some cervical cancers, breast cancers, barrenness, miscarriages, and fibroids can be traced to abortion as the stronghold.

We have had situations where people have come to us because of a totally unrelated situation. As we begin the process of deliverance, it turns out that the Lord reveals the root cause as abortion. This has necessitated that we help the person receive forgiveness from abortion. One woman came to me in uttermost privacy and advised me that they had an abortion. She also stated that she helped recommend an abortion for another woman. This made her feel responsible for the death of both babies. The weight of guilt and shame for this sin weighed on her so much that she had begun to develop a shame-based identity. She could not fully step into her place of inheritance and call of God for her life. The enemy was constantly reminding her of her sin.

It is quite disturbing to note that a lot of abortions are from evangelical Christians that on one hand will vote pro-life as a political stand. But when confronted with a personal situation of an unplanned pregnancy, they do not see any other way forward. The fear of having the baby disrupt their lives leads them to choosing abortion as the only option. In a situation like this, the woman in their heart of hearts is conflicted with having to do something that they know is evil and sinful. To have to push hard against their conscience leads to a place where the heart becomes callous. Such an inner turmoil is like a living hell. Human beings are not created to live under that amount of inner turmoil. Most people after the abortion they slide into the deep dark pit of depression and desperation. It is at that point that most people begin looking for help either through healing or deliverance ministry.

The first thing I do when I meet with someone is to make sure to get them at ease. Abortion is not the unpardonable sin. It can be forgiven. But the person needs to come before God, confess their sin and completely repent of it. I allow the person to pray a very simple prayer of repentance. Then we begin to deal with the guilt, the shame, and the condemnation. There are some people riddled and tormented by the enemy in secret. A lot of the weight of the torment is because they haven't confessed openly about the sin. Whenever a sin is confessed publicly, it loses its power. Secret sins can only thrive in secrecy. When the cover of secrecy is removed through confession, the sin loses its power to shame the person. In fact, what I have experienced is the complete opposite. After the secret sins are uncovered, the Lord empowers us to boldly speak of his forgiveness and grace. It also opens the door for people who were secretly being tormented by the devil to come out in the open and receive their freedom. It is such vulnerable moments that open up a platform to minister to others. Whenever I become vulnerable, others become vulnerable too, and in the process, God brings such a deep healing. During the repentance, we repent to God for taking the life of the child whose destiny was aborted. We repent for terminating the life and the purpose of someone created in the image of God. Through the act of repentance, we also plead the blood of Jesus on our conscience. That way, every callousness of our conscience is cleansed by the blood of Jesus. It is also through the repentance that we get our heart to come back to alignment with God's heart. That way, God can use the person again to birth forth his purposes through future offsprings. We use this time to plead the blood on the family lineage and cleanse the family from the scourge of abortion. Always remember, abortion is not just a sin. It is an iniquity that becomes the basis of a generational curse. When innocent blood is shed, the enemy can lay a claim to the future generations. It is very vital that you silence the mouth of the accuser by pleading the blood of Jesus on the future generations. Make sure to stop abortion from spreading to the next generation. Don't let it become an open door for the spirit of death, miscarriages or infirmity. Do not take any chances. Cover all the bases with the blood of Jesus.

Finally, forgive yourself and let yourself off the hook. Use this to lift off all forms of guilt, shame, condemnation, and self-blame. I have learned to not allow the enemy to shame me. God has promised me that I'll never be put to shame. Be very intentional to refuse to carry any form of shame. There are some things that you have done, but they are not you. Performing an abortion does not make you a murderer. You're a new creation in Christ. Once you're forgiven, there is no more condemnation for you. It is as if you never did anything wrong. Walk with your head high. You're not even an ex-abortionist. You're not ex anything! You're a new creation in Christ. The old man that aborted is now dead and buried. The new you has been raised from the dead and now lives for Jesus. Embrace forgiveness. Receive full pardon. Act like it. Know you're it.

PRACTICING FORGIVENESS THERAPY IN HEALING MINISTRY.

Several years ago, we were conducting a healing campaign in the State of Indiana, USA. There came a woman who was in a wheelchair. That night, the power of God was flowing like liquid fire. I mean, people were getting healed left, right and center. There are times healing ministry flows so unrestricted that you can literally see all the people in the room healed. But them all over sudden, we got to this one woman, and it was like romanticizing a stone. I mean, complete total shutdown of the flow of the power of God. Sometimes you'll encounter that wall of resistance. It is like trying to take a territory, and suddenly you have this fortified building that is a castle with thick, impenetrable walls. That is called a stronghold. It simply means that the enemy has a foothold and has built a stronghold on a yielded territory. Paul tells the Ephesians not to give any room to the devil. That also means, not to yield any legal ground. The reason is simple. When Satan gets a legal ground yielded, he'll use it to build a stronghold.

In this situation, the stronghold was unforgiveness. It had caused severe arthritis to a point where this woman was in a wheelchair. After repentance, she miraculously got healed.

In my ministry across America and around the world, I deal with so many cases of sickness that are due to Unforgiveness. In one of the most successful crusades I have ever done in the State of Minnesota, USA, we went through the teaching of removing the legal ground of unforgiveness. When I began to pray, only a handful of people got healed. I took all those who were not healed. I put them into a section all by themselves. I knew by the Holy Spirit that if we go through forgiveness therapy, we shall see a lot of miracles and healing take place.

Then I asked them to think of 3 to 5 people they need to forgive. I gave them one minute to mention their names before the Lord and under their breath. I asked them to completely lay those names before the Lord and let them go. Oh my God! The outcome was unreal. We had people forgive their fathers, offenders, rapists, business colleagues, spouses, family members, and friends. The results were incredible glory and grace fell into the room. A young lady who had been abused began going through massive deliverance right after forgiveness. She began vomiting blood. Suddenly miracles began breaking out. People were shaking under the power of God. His glory was flowing in and through them. I can say that that was the night we saw the greatest of the move of God. Cripples walked, deaf ears opened, cancers were healed, tumors vanished, blind eyes opened, and a lot of deliverances took place. When you know the power of forgiveness, healing is easy.

I was in the State of Wisconsin. I taught on the same subject. A young lady in the room began shaking and manifesting demonic spirits. She suddenly began to become borderline violent, cursing, swearing and throwing chairs. But she continued pressing on with the prayer in spite of the demonic manifestations happening through her. By the end of the service, she was gloriously set free by the power of God. You should have seen the beautiful smile on her face! God gave her so much joy back and peace from the tormenting spirits. In my opinion, unforgiveness is the biggest stronghold of all in the church. While only a handful has shed innocent blood or involved in magic or witchcraft, most people have grudges of Unforgiveness, and they haven't dealt with it.

In some situations, it is not easy for people to forgive. Of course, not everyone is ready to let go of their grudge. Some people are not quite there in their understanding of forgiveness. There are definitely people who feel justified to stay angry and to feel the way they do towards their offenders.

This being the case, I have encountered a few people who do not want to forgive. In both cases, they were victims of rape. It also happened to them when they were little. I definitely cannot relate to their situation. I cannot also imagine how they feel. I probably understand a little of their concern. Both of them screamed at me and said, "I'll not forgive them! I wish they rot in prison and burn in hell". For such a person, it is not possible to help them. I only pray that the Lord would reveal to them the need for forgiveness and help them do it by the power of the Holy Spirit. Without the forgiveness, there cannot be healing.

I have ministered to thousands of people on this subject, and it doesn't stop amazing me. Recently I was ministering at our church. I shared on how prayers are answered easier when we forgive. I encouraged people to close the door of Unforgiveness and begin practicing forgiveness therapy. I had people come to me and say how freeing it has been. Someone who had carried deep shame for over ten years was suddenly set free. They came to me at the end of the service and were so moved by the amount of freedom they felt. Someone else who was dealing with an incurable disease began to share with me that they believe that my message on that day was the key they needed for their healing. A lot of people are carrying so much garbage of toxic emotions. Some of it is manifesting as sickness and disease. When we let go and forgive, it is the beginning of a new and exciting chapter of life. Allow the cleansing river of forgiveness to begin flowing into your life. It is such a very refreshing and life-giving experience.

HOW DID THIS HAPPEN?

Here are the 7 steps that you can take right now to experience the same outcome like Liz did.

1. Recognize:

Recognize the root of what you're dealing with. Always understand that for everything, there's cause and effect. When you see the effect, most likely it will point to the cause. God is faithful to reveal the root. If you cannot recognize the cause, pray in a general way that God would render all causes completely powerless. He's faithful.

2. Repent:

Repent of all the sins, iniquities and transgressions. Apply the blood of Jesus in your life and let God bring you to a place of peace with himself, yourself and others.

3. Renounce:

Renounce all the works of darkness that have given Satan any entry point in our lives. What doors have you opened through your words and deeds? Severe the ties. Cut the cord of connection. The word of God reminds us not to give any foothold to the devil.

4. Resist:

Resist the devil, and he will flee from you. Use your authority in the name of Jesus, the blood of Jesus, the word of God and put Satan where he belongs. His place is under our feet. You too can experience total victory in your life.

5. Restore:

Restore all that has been stolen. Learn how to speak everything back to its place. Learn how to speak life, speak the true destiny of God into a situation. Always restore hope with the words of your mouth. Forgiveness is always the beginning of a new day of a new beginning. Speak it into being.

6. Repeat:

Repeat the process if necessary. Sometimes it will take you more than once to get the desired outcome. Always remember that persistence breaks resistance. Many times in the Bible, the answer came after praying for 7 times. Nobody knows how long it will take. But never give up. Keep praying until something happens.

CHAPTER 6

HOW FORGIVENESS THERAPY WORKS

HOW TO FORGIVE; THE 7 SIMPLE STEPS TO A NEW BEGINNING.

1. **See unforgiveness for what it is.** Hate it. Get sick and tired of it. Call it what it is. It is a poison meant to kill you unless you choose to get rid of it.

Here are the damages that unforgiveness will do to a person;

i) It opens the door for the tormentors to come in.

Read Matthew 18:23-35, and keep in mind that the tormenters they are referring to, are demons. The legal ground the enemy may be standing on to torment you may very well be rooted in unforgiveness! I've heard that the single most common reason that people aren't healed is because they are holding unforgiveness in their hearts, and I believe it!

ii) It leads to vulnerability to sickness and diseases.

Prov 17:22-

A cheerful heart is a good medicine, but a crushed spirit dries up the bones.

iii) It hinders prayers from being answered

1 Peter 3:7-Likewise, ye husbands, dwell with them according to knowledge, giving honor unto the wife, as unto the weaker vessel, and as being heirs together of the grace of life; that your prayers be not hindered

iv) God refuses to forgive those who refuse to forgive.

v) unforgiveness can lead to physical death and eternal separation from God. I know of a man who had a heart attack. He died on the spot as a result of being in a bitter, heated argument with one of his family members. That family had so many piles of unresolved conflicts. On that fateful day, it was like the last straw. We don't know where the dead man went. But we know he died a bitter man.

I believe when we come to terms with the damage of unforgiveness, we shall appreciate the need of letting go. Sometimes we hang on the offenses and unforgiveness because we don't quite see the reality. Sleeping with the enemy is the worst thing you can do to yourself. Unforgiveness is like the man who kept on sleeping with the proverbial snake. At the opportune time, the snake administered a fatal bite. As the man was dying, he screamed and asked the snake how dare it bites him after he has been so nice to it. The snake responded by calling him stupid and naive. The last words of the snake to the dying man was, "you knew before you let me on your bed that I was a poisonous snake and you still let me in."

2. **Always forgive by choice.** Make sure to remember that God has placed in front of us choices. He places death and life as a matter of choice. He tells us to choose life, and we shall live. Part of choosing life is knowing how to embrace the choice of forgiveness. Here are the 3 benefits to consider;

   i) Because God commands us to do so it's good we do it.

   ii) Because you recognize that you have been totally forgiven the only choice is to forgive others.

   iii) It is the right thing to do. You can never go wrong or miss God by choosing to forgive.

God saved you by grace—not because you deserved it (Eph. 2:1-10). He has freely offered His forgiveness to you.

3. **Confess it to God and ask Him to release you.** Take 3 minutes of silence. Reflect on this subject of forgiveness. Ask God a very simple question;

   i) "Father God, show me all the names of people that I need to forgive. Bring them to my memory so that I can let them go."

ii) Immediately, begin writing or mentioning those names (under your breath or loudly). As you do this, a lot of burdens will begin to fall off.

iii) Say these words; Father in the name of Jesus, I let go of _____ from my heart. I totally release them from any Unforgiveness.

iv) As soon as you mention the name(s), spontaneously release them and know it is done.

v) You may feel something or nothing at all. That doesn't matter. If you have forgiven, it is done. The feelings will follow your intentional quality decision.

vi) Release the other person from what you believe he or she owes you for the offense.

vii) Take any hostile feelings you may have and willingly surrender them to Christ. Just say these words, "I now surrender all the hostile emotions to Christ."

Whose job is it to get revenge (Rom. 12:19)? It is the Lord. Put the matter in His hands.

Your biggest assignment is to love others, and that's all you need to focus on. That's why this is a great opportunity for you to confess your anger to God.

If the person is alive, you may want to reach out to them. If they are dead, do it anyway and let it go.

4. PUT OFF...This is what you intentionally do.

Here are the attitudes that Paul instruct us to "put off."

(Eph. 4:30-32): [31]Get rid of all bitterness, rage, and anger, brawling and slander, along with every form of malice. [32]Be kind and compassionate to one another, forgiving each other, just as in Christ God forgave you.

Say it out loud;

"as an act of my will, I want to be intentional about forgiveness and putting off the old nature. I choose to get rid of all bitterness, rage, and anger, brawling and slander, along with every form of malice. I choose to be kind and compassionate to others, forgiving each other, just as in Christ God forgave me. This choice has nothing to do with how I feel or what I like. It is a simple obedience and desire to live by the principle of forgiveness. I consider it done in Jesus name"

5. PUT ON...

This also is an act of choice, motivated by our will and intentionality.

We choose to "put on" (Col. 3:12-17)

[12]Therefore, as God's chosen people, holy and dearly loved, clothe yourselves with compassion, kindness, humility, gentleness and patience. [13]Bear with each other and forgive one another if any of you has a grievance against someone. Forgive as the Lord forgave you. [14]And over all these virtues put on love, which binds them all together in perfect unity.

[15]Let the peace of Christ rule in your hearts, since as members of one body you were called to peace. And be thankful. [16]Let the message of Christ dwell among you richly as you teach and admonish one another with all wisdom through psalms, hymns, and songs from the Spirit, singing to God with gratitude in your hearts. [17]And whatever you do, whether in word or deed, do it all in the name of the Lord Jesus, giving thanks to God the Father through him.

The best place to start from is by making this confession;

"Because I am forgiven, chosen and loved by God, I put on myself compassion, kindness, humility, gentleness and patience. I choose to forgive and bear with others if they have a grievance against me. I choose to forgive just as I have been forgiven. And over all these virtues I put on love, which binds everything and everyone together in perfect unity.

6. See it as a necessary evil.

The Lord uses the difficult situations we experience to refine our character and sharpen us spiritually (Rom. 8:28-29). Many times we, like Joseph, can see how God used adversity to arrange the circumstances of our lives for His purposes

JOSEPH LEARNT TO NOT REVENGE BUT FORGIVE.

"'Thus you shall say to Joseph: "I beg you, please forgive the trespass of your brothers and their sin; for they did evil to you." 'Now, please, forgive the trespass of the servants of the God of your father." And Joseph wept when they spoke to him. Then his brothers also went and fell down before his face, and they said, "Behold, we are your servants." Joseph said to them, "Do not be afraid, for am I in the place of God? But as for you, you meant evil against me; but God meant it for good, in order to bring it about as it is this day, to save many people alive. Now, therefore, do not be afraid; I will provide for you and your little ones." And he comforted them and spoke kindly to them." Genesis 50:17-21 NKJV

Some of the most painful experiences are going to be used to teach us the greatest lessons of our lives.

Jesus on the cross chose forgiveness. He knew those who betrayed and crucified Him were part of the big picture of the necessary evil to bring to fruition the plan of redemption.

Luke 23:34 says, "Father forgive them for they do not know what they are doing."

7. **Open a new chapter on a clean slate.** When you pass the test of forgiveness, you are ready for promotion and new open doors. We receive the prize of the mark of our high calling when we learn to forget the past.

Philippians 3:13 Brothers and sisters, I do not consider myself yet to have taken hold of it. But one thing I do: Forgetting what is behind and straining toward what is ahead, 14 I press on toward the goal to win the prize for which God has called me heavenward in Christ Jesus.

Only through forgiveness can we find genuine freedom from bitterness, resentment, and anger. Release your hostile feelings to the Lord, and allow His presence to heal and restore you.

Pray along with me:

"Heavenly Father, my natural tendency is to hold onto hurt and anger. Please grant me the grace to extend forgiveness to others because of the amazing mercy you have shown me. In Jesus' name, I pray. Amen."

CHAPTER 7

HOW YOU KNOW THAT YOU KNOW YOU'VE FORGIVEN.

I t is very easy to doubt and second guess yourself after you're done with the process of forgiveness. Don't be overly concerned when your emotions refuse to adjust at the same speed with your intentional choice to forgive. This is a normal progressional curve. When I gave my life to Jesus, the experience was epic. Sometimes way too overwhelming for my emotions to handle. My intellect was a little hesitant to jump on the bandwagon of the euphoria that was going on in my emotional realm. I had to consistently and repeatedly remind myself that I am saved, and it has actually happened. It came from being surreal to real. This transition from being bitter and vindictive to being healed and loving may not be an overnight thing. For some, it may mean walking those baby steps and taking one day at a time.

For the most part, there will be a voice in your head that will put up an intense inner dialogue. Do not be alarmed if such an inner dialogue breaks out in you after you forgive. Those voices will create inner tension. They will question the validity of your choice. They will make it hard for you to believe that you have truly forgiven. That voice is not of God. That is the voice of the enemy. It carries with it guilt, shame, condemnation, hopelessness, helplessness, and accusations. It puts you down and drags you back to the past. You probably are not accustomed to such intense spiritual warfare. Do not allow it to throw you off your game. Stay with your choice of forgiveness no matter what. I promise you, that voice though intense cannot outlive your faith to stand strong.

The Bible tells us to expect this kind of spiritual warfare. Always remember, spiritual warfare is part of our daily experience. The battlefield is our mind. You win this battle by speaking God's word of truth to the circumstances. The stronger the warfare, the louder your voice should be to reaffirm and remind yourself that you have already forgiven. You need to keep speaking until you finally silence the mouth of the accuser. There's no telling when else the enemy will raise his ugly head again. But keep up with your plan of action to move forward in forgiveness, and the more you do it, the more your faith will prevail over all the voices in your head. Starve the voice of the accuser. Don't let it play you.

"Do not allow the voices in your head to get you out of your game. Stay the course and forgive regardless of how you feel" (Dr.Charles)

Let your forgiveness be guided by the principle and not by the feelings. If you wait for your feelings to lead your decisions to forgive, it may never happen. After all, do you want a feeling or a healing? The choice is yours.

Here are the 10 ways you can know you have truly forgiven.

1. Because you did it in accordance with God's word and expect the results in accordance with the word of God.

2. Because you did it as an act of your will in obedience to what God requires. Never second guess yourself. It will invite more doubts.

3. Your forgiveness unlocks blessings and allows your prayer to be answered. Ask God to give you a sign of progress as evidence that you have truly forgiven. God is faithful. He will let it happen.

4. You will have no more pain after you're done forgiving. The bitterness in your soul will be healed, and you will be the first to feel that the weight is off your shoulders.

5. There will be the increase of the fruit of love. It will grow and flow in and through you and others will

feel it. You may hear from your family and friends testify to the impact of your walk of love.

6. You will begin to sense a greater sense of joy rising in your soul. Depression will be broken, and sorrowful cycles of grief will fall off your life.

7. God will give you so much peace. This is a sense of tranquility and settling in the inside. You will be more tame, settled, relaxed, confident, less frigidly and more comfortable inside your skin. This will also mean out of control cycles of worry and anxiety attacks will be broken off from your life.

8. Watch for the way you respond to others. After you are done forgiving, expect to grow in self-control. You will be slow to anger and very gracious. You will be harder to set off into a rage of temper tantrums. The natural outcome of forgiveness is becoming rich in love, grace, and mercy.

9. A big sign of how much you have forgiven is that the levels of toxic emotions begin to fall significantly. You no longer have the tight knots and spells of pain in your belly. You feel more at ease emotionally. (Make sure to take the test on measuring your toxic levels; see the back of the book)

10. I have noticed people who have truly forgiven are also very gentle, humble and meek. It is like the fight is removed from them. Their instincts of fight

or flight are no longer at elevated levels. That is what self-control is all about. The fruit of it is manifested in the way we walk in gentleness with others.

FREE YOUR EMOTIONAL HARD DRIVE. GET READY TO LOAD NEW AND UPGRADED SOFTWARE INTO YOUR SYSTEM.

NOW GET READY FOR A SEASON OF ACCELERATION.

3 John 2: Beloved, I pray/ wish above all things that you may prosper and be in health even as your soul prospers.

What you'll realize is that for the first time in a long while, you're free. Your soul is free from toxic emotions that have limited your ability to prosper. Now the room that had been taken by the pain and bitterness is now ready to be filled with new and brighter ideas. I think of this process as a way of cleaning a computer hard drive. Sometimes we clean up the old junk files that had taken the space and slowed down the computer's functionality.

It is time to hit the delete button. Sometimes my iPhone gets very slow. It is because I have allowed old pictures and videos to fill up the memory space in the hard drive and slow the speed. As soon as that space is freed up, now we can download new and faster software that literary reboots the whole system to give my phone a brand new beginning. I believe it is time to delete some old files, photos, videos and free your emotional space for greater clarity and better days.

Get ready for a new season of open doors, acceleration, increase, and prosperity. New relationships, better relationships, new and fresh ideas and new mindsets. Get ready for a new world view not colored by our toxic emotions. Know that a new fragrance is coming from your inside. You'll be able to sustain relationships and keep great friends. You'll be able to relate to the healed and minister to the wounded.

5 SIMPLE REQUIREMENTS FOR EFFECTIVE FORGIVENESS THERAPY.

1. **Do it quickly and unconditionally.** Proceed with or without feelings. Make it as an act of your will. Don't give it time to defile your emotions.

You've heard people say that time heals. The truth of the matter is time does not heal. What time does, it puts things under the carpet and at the opportune time, they will explode in the most destructive manner you can ever imagine. Time can work against you. It can cause the roots of bitterness to go very deep and defile your life. Here are a few reminders.

Delayed obedience is disobedience.

Delayed forgiveness leads to a root of bitterness growing and may defile many.

Remember the 12hr rule. Don't allow the sun to go down while you're still angry. Move quickly and get a closure. This rule keeps marriages free from the build up of unresolved conflicts. Do it seven times seven each day. Make it a lifestyle. Let every moment count.

Use your will as a weapon. You have control over your will. Take advantage of that self-control. Use it to control your focus and dominant thoughts. When it steers your mind in a certain direction, the rest of your being will follow. As long as your will is aligned with the will of God, He will support your actions. Someone said that of you get addicted to doing what pleases God, He will support your habit. Your will in agreement with the will of God will cause the power of the Holy Spirit to move and bring forth the miraculous.

2. **Obey and forgive regardless of the feelings.** Feelings can change. They should never be trusted to lead. Make it a matter of choosing the right thing. Do you want healing or just following your feelings? Do the right thing. Let the feelings adjust later. Remember forgiveness is an act of your will not of your feelings.

3. **Draw healthy boundaries to protect yourself in the future.** Do not allow someone to keep coming in and out to hurt you. In some cases, you need to remove yourself from the situation where you're constantly being hurt.

4. **Make it a lifestyle and watch your quality of life go very high.** Welcome to a new way of living. It's better here. Once you taste the lifestyle of forgiveness, you'll never want it any other way.

5. **Forgive yourself.** Forgive others. Then love God through it all. Life is too short to live it in bitterness and emotional pain. Choose to enjoy the boundless joy and abundant life. Keep your heart and soul pure. Detox your soul often. Stay free from toxic emotions. Don't postpone your best days to sometimes after. Make today the best day of your life. Go through life with a smile on your face and a joyful heart.

HOW TAKING COMMUNION CAN TRIGGER YOUR HEALING.

I now know why communion is popularly referred to as the meal that heals. One of the keys to taking communion is self-examination. Paul admonishes the Corinthians to examine themselves before partaking of the table of the Lord (communion). Proper self-examination means letting go of others that have transgressed you. As often as you partake of communion, you give yourself the opportunity to self-examine.

We have heard stories after stories of people who got healed after adopting the habit of taking communion every day. Some people have attributed taking communion every day as the secret to their good health and longevity. Others have been healed of incurable diseases after beginning to take communion every day. At the heart of that healing is the self-examination that comes through forgiveness.

Paul outlines the entire concept of communion in his letter to the Corinthians.

> "For I received from the Lord that which I also delivered to you: that the Lord Jesus on the same night in which He was betrayed took bread; and when He had given thanks, He broke it and said, "Take, eat; this is My body which is broken for you; do this in remembrance of Me." In the same manner, He also took the cup after supper, saying, "This cup is the new covenant in My blood. This does, as often as you drink it, in remembrance of Me." For as often as you eat this bread and drink this cup, you proclaim the Lord's death till He comes. Therefore whoever eats this bread or drinks this cup of the Lord in an unworthy manner will be guilty of the body and blood of the Lord. But let a man examine himself, and so let him eat of the bread and drink of the cup. For he who eats and drinks in an unworthy manner eats and drinks judgment to himself, not discerning the Lord's body. For this reason, many are weak and sick among you, and many sleep. For if we would judge ourselves, we would not be judged." I Corinthians 11:23-31 NKJV

Here is a breakdown of this teaching.

1. We partake of the communion in remembrance of Him. This remembrance points to the finished work of Jesus on the cross. It is the remembrance of the blood, the covenant we have with God, the forgiveness of our debt of sins, the new life we have in the Lord and fact that the blood of Jesus has provided for the penalty of our sins. Upon remembrance of this finished work of Jesus on the cross, we can receive the perspective of how we have been forgiven and therefore making it easier to forgive others.

2. There's no limit of how often we should partake of the communion. The Bible says we do it "often." That means as much as you're able to do. I know of people who partake communion seven times a day on some occasions. Taking communion at least once a day and making it a habit of your life can be the most healthy decision you've ever taken. People who take communion often do not give room for evil plans to build up in their inside.

3. Communion involves partaking of the blood and the body of Jesus. The blood is for the cleansing of our sins while the body is for healing and strength. Many times we get tired and burnt out in the journey. It is the strength of the blood and the body of

Jesus that can keep us going from day to day. Elijah was told by the Lord to arise and eat in preparation for a journey of forty days. The same was the case with the children of Israel. They partook of the Passover meal, which is a type of communion, in preparation for their forty-year journey through the wilderness. The results were phenomenon. Their clothes and shoes never grew old while in the wilderness. There was no feeble (sick) among them. God filled them with supernatural life to help the weather through the harsh life of the wilderness.

We haven't taken the concept of pleading the blood of Jesus seriously. The power of the blood of Jesus is to cleanse us as white as snow. It restores our position of righteousness. It gives us unlimited access to the throne of God. On the basis of the blood, we are able to go boldly into the throne of grace and obtain mercy and help in the time of need. The blood is our ultimate weapon of victory over sin, sickness, disease, demons, guilt, shame and condemnation. It is the blood that washes us of all the impurities and allows us to become spotless and unashamed to take our place as joint heirs in Christ. Whenever you partake of the communion, allow the blood of Jesus to cleanse you of any legal rights the enemy may use against you. Let the blood of Jesus go through your veins into your blood and let it fill up your DNA. This revelation has the power to heal blood disorders, break generational curses and put in us the very blood of Jesus which is the blood of God his father! That way, we begin to manifest the royal lineage we carry as true sons of the King of kings and the Lord of lords. What a power in the blood!

1. Communion should never be taken in an unworthy manner. The meal that heals can also be the meal that kills! The Bible warns that those who refuse to examine themselves of sin and unrighteousness are in danger of partaking the communion in an unworthy manner. The consequences of refusing to examine oneself are sickness, weakness, and premature death. These three things are similar to what unforgiveness and bitterness can do. I'm convinced that letting go of bitterness is the way to allow God to truly bring us to a healthy place from which we can obtain great victories. The church is sick because of unforgiveness. But the meal that heals gives us an opportunity to experience the healing grace of God. I pray you'll never partake of communion in the same way again.

2. At the communion table, it is a place of discerning the Lord's body. I have wondered what that truly means. I believe we are to look at the body of Jesus at the cross and see how he was wounded and pierced for our sin as well as to bring forth the

Church. Always remember the broken body of Jesus before partaking of the communion. It is a place where we remember that Jesus was pierced on his side and out of that would come put water and blood. This was the same thing that happened to Adam in the garden. God opened him on his side and out of the broken side of Adam, Eve was created. When Jesus was pierced, as the last Adam, he gave birth to a New Testament bride, called the Church. The message of communion is that we rightly discern the body of Christ. It is a word of caution to those who dishonor the church, speak evil of the church, speak evil of the leadership of the church or those who wound the church through divisions and gossips. There's a need for the people in the church to always be in a place of self-examination regarding the way we are treating the bride of Christ. Sometimes it is so easy to speak loosely and dishonorably against the church. Such a treacherous treatment to the body of Christ can be corrected during communion. As we are examining ourselves before the Lord, we can allow him to roll those sins away.

3. Communion is a place of judging ourselves so that we don't have to be judged. I love the concept of self-judgment. People who self-judge are able to

preempt an outsider from judging them. The easiest way to judge yourself during communion is to take that moment of silence to stand before the spotlight of heaven and allow God to shine it brightly right through your heart. The spotlight of heaven makes everything transparent and naked before him like what x-ray does. You're able to see the hidden parts and how they look. This spotlight reveals to redeem. When you tell God to show you yourself, He is faithful and just and will reveal to you the condition of your heart. One of the things I ask him all the time is to bring to my attention people that I have not forgiven. Throughout my decades of a walk with Him, God has always given me 3-5 names of people that I should let go in His presence.

4. Communion time is also a time of speaking and enforcing the blessings and benefits of the covenant of the finished work of Jesus on the cross. What we focus on we magnify. What we magnify we attract. When we learn to focus and magnify on over three thousand covenant blessings of salvation, we are able to begin to partake of them. It is during the communion that we experience the fullness of the word salvation (sozo). It means being forgiven, healed, delivered, filled with the love of God,

blessed, prospered and fully loaded with the heavenly benefits. It is a place of thriving and breaking off every chain of darkness. This is not a place we should rush through. It is a place we should camp, dwell and build a home. It is a place where we should spiritually marinate until we soak in all the juices of our covenant relationship with God.

There are many things I recommend for forgiveness therapy. Apart from praying for those that have offended you, partaking of communion is a way to minister to yourself in ways that bring out the best in you. Sometimes, there are things that have become so difficult, and nothing else can do. By partaking of communion often, we are able to cause all the strongholds to come down.

CHAPTER 8

UNDERSTANDING WHAT FORGIVENESS IS.

To pardon, exonerate, extend mercy. This is regardless of whether the offender has asked for it or not. It is regardless of whether the offender is alive or dead.

Forgiveness is for your own benefit. It cleanses your heart and mind from toxic emotions that are very detrimental to your health and wellbeing.

Extending forgiveness to others just as God has forgiven us is in our best of interest.

It is JESUS who taught us to forgive others of transgressions as we forgive those who transgress AGAINST us Matt 6:12.

5 THINGS THAT FORGIVENESS IS NOT.

1. **Does not always mean reconcile, trust and be friends.** Sometimes it means loving them from a distance. It may mean getting new friends that are more functional. However, before you move on, forgive.

2. **Does not mean open yourself to repeatedly being abused.** Forgiveness does not mean letting them walk all over you. Be wise and seek for healthy and functional relationships. Make sure to draw healthy boundaries. Begin attracting healthy people that know how to relate better. Get yourself people that add value to your life. Find positive people that are going somewhere. Keep yourself great company.

3. **Does not stop the pursuit of earthly justice. Sometimes the law has to take its cause.** Even someone whom God has forgiven can be prosecuted for crimes committed before they were forgiven. If the law wants to catch up with them, that's totally understandable.

Forgiveness puts the issue in the hands of God. It's not our place to determine how he deals with it. Vengeance is of God. Let him repay.

4. **It does not mean forgetting.** All it means is that you forget the feelings of bitterness, anger, resentment

and all the toxic emotions associated with it. Forgiveness does not erase your memory of the past. It just means that you will share about your past memories with a smile on your face and a heart that overflows with the love of God. There's an incredible healing of the memories and the pain associated with those things that happened. It means the root of bitterness has been removed. When the bitter roots come out, you're no longer under the poisonous venom of unforgiveness. That's where you want to be.

5. **Forgiveness is not because we are weak.** To the contrary, it is a demonstration of our strength. It is because we are meek. It comes out of a choice to demonstrate our strength under control. It shows everyone how we are able to keep our emotions in check despite all the provocation. Jesus although he was the Lion of the tribe of Judah, he chose to be a lamb. He demonstrated to us the ultimate strength of his meekness and humility. At the end of it all, he overcame all his enemies plots and all the adversity in his life. You too can have the same victory if you believe in the power of forgiveness.

When Nelson Mandela came out of prison, we all expected him to revenge. After all, the white South African governments had put him in prison for 27 years. They had taken all his prime life. He had lost and missed out in tens of thousands of days of quality time with family and friends. Many people were telling him to use the political power that he had to get even. However, Mandela decided to exercise restraint by forgiving. That was the reason why South Africa did not go into a civil war. A worse outcome was averted through forgiveness. Those who forgive are the stronger ones. That's why today we are still talking of Nelson Mandela. May you too be remembered among the greatest because of your love for forgiveness.

APPLYING FORGIVENESS THERAPY AFTER GENOCIDE.

It is easier said than done. Forgiving after genocide takes more than mere words. The reason is simple. War is hell. But genocide is hell on steroids. I look at genocide as the spirit of murder let loose to run rampant and wreak all the havoc with maximum destruction possible. It's like getting an entire population to become demon possessed, then arm them with blunt objects and machetes, and then set them loose on each other. Genocide is when the human instincts are suspended, and then the animal instinct is hyper stimulated and allowed to run amok. The world watched with folded arms as Rwanda went into a free fall into the abyss of the greatest human slaughter ever witnessed in Africa. Even the rivers of human blood and stench of piles of rotting human bodies never caught the attention of the world busy with the dot com boom of the 90s.

In Rwanda of 1994, ethnic cleansing of the minority Tutsi by the majority Hutu was the reason why close to one million people were killed. Imagine a country where there was no single person who did not either lose a father, mother, brother, sister, cousin, nephew, niece, grandparents, friend or neighbor. It was this level of bitterness and rage that fueled the genocide. Everyone was paranoid and on the edge. Everyone was on a mission to revenge, protect themselves and do their best to not trust others. Family, friends, and neighbors turned into foes. Friends turned swords on friends. Neighbors betrayed neighbors into their death traps. People turned blunt objects and machetes into weapons. Rape, arson, torture, carnage and brutal force were unleashed against anyone of the opposite tribal descent. Some of the most graphic stories of trials and triumphs are still being told today. More astronomical than the carnage of the hell-like horrors of genocide is the trail of terror and devastation left behind. The trauma of the survivors, the widows, widowers, orphans and displaced people of Rwanda is something probably never witnessed before. I wanted to include some stories from a few journalists who interviewed some of the perpetrators as well as the victims. You'll be touched by both sides of the perspectives and also see how forgiveness therapy was applied to heal the nation. Today, Rwanda is one of the fastest growing economies in the world! I believe their ability to practice national healing and reconciliation is the secret to their meteoric rise from the ashes of ruin, doom, and gloom.

Here are some stories from Rwanda.

Aline Umegwaneza: Aline Umegwaneza: forgiving genocide.

Christine McWhorter - 700 Club Producer

CBN.com -April 6, 1994, marked the beginning of one of the bloodiest chapters in Rwandan history. After Tutsi rebels had assassinated Rwanda's president, the government responded brutally with the genocide of an estimated 800,000 people – most of them civilians.

Aline Umegwaneza shares her story. "My name is Aline. I was 16 when the genocide began in Rwanda. It was very scary. It was very sad. We did not have hope."

Armed with machetes and guns, government soldiers went from house to house, looking for traitors. "Every minute, day by day, they killed people. During that time, that's when our mom told us to pack up what we need - different clothes. We didn't want the people to come during the night to kill us."

Aline and her family fled their village in the early morning hours. Her mom stopped to help a neighbor and said she would catch up with Aline and her younger siblings later. Soon after, Aline witnessed the unthinkable. "That's when I started to hear the noise of guns. They shoot. One person dies here. You see another person die there."

"Then that's when I saw women were running to save their lives. They leave their little kids. You hear kids crying on the street. Babies, one year, two months, three months - because the people run to save their lives."

Hours later, Aline still hadn't seen her mother. "That's when I start to get desperate. I start to see <u>at 6 pm</u> and no mom. I only see bodies. I start to think, 'I think she died.'" Aline found out later that her mom had been murdered.

To stay alive, she and her siblings had to keep moving. They hid in different houses until finally, they found a refugee camp. But even there, they weren't safe. "During the camp life - the camp life was bad. They were killing each other. So we were waiting to die anytime in the camp."

After only 3 months, the conflict was over. Aline returned home with her siblings and took in a family whose house had been destroyed. But the family wanted Aline's property for themselves. One day when Aline was away, the family killed her brothers and sisters. "They killed them."

Aline knew that if she didn't leave, she would be next. So she went on the run again, with no idea where to go. She ran into an old classmate, whose family took her in. "It was a good family. They are wealthy. They have everything. We used to go to the lake. They had money. But, we lost over 75 members of my family, alone. I was angry at that time for losing my people. I had this bit of bitterness in me."

Aline bonded with the girl's mother, Sylvia, who told her about Jesus. Soon, Aline began going to church. She accepted Christ as her Savior, but she was still bitter toward the people who murdered her family. She tried again and again to forgive, but couldn't. "Every time I go to the church, they speak about forgiveness. I said, 'What about the people who have killed my family, my siblings, the people who burned my mom alive, the people who cut my family into pieces, who crushed my siblings with a stone and crushed their head like a snake?'"

Aline says she was finally able to forgive them when she read a verse in the Bible. "I used to think I was the one who is right. They were wrong. Until I read Matthew 6:14-15, 'If you don't forgive others, God will not forgive you.'"

Aline says afterward God gave her peace she never had before. Today, she's a missionary and a preacher. She believes that no matter what has been done to you, Christ can help you forgive.

"After forgiving those people completely, I started to help other people. It's like joy came in my life. I have a joy inside of me… And compassion – before I did not have compassion. Today I help the people around the world, different nations."

"Jesus set me free."

http://www1.cbn.com/700club/aline-umegwaneza-forgiving-genocide

---

SINZIKIRAMUKA, PERPETRATOR: "I asked him for forgiveness because his brother was killed in my presence. He asked me why I pleaded guilty, and I replied that I did it as someone who witnessed this crime but who was unable to save anybody. It was the order from authorities. I let him know who the killers were, and the killers also asked him for pardon."

KARORERO, SURVIVOR: "Sometimes justice does not give someone a satisfactory answer — cases are subject to corruption. But when it comes to forgiveness willingly granted, one is satisfied once and for all. When someone is full of anger, he can lose his mind. But when I granted forgiveness, I felt my mind at rest."

Jean Pierre Karenzi *perpetrator*, Viviane Nyiramana, survivor.

KARENZI: "My conscience was not quiet, and when I would see her I was very ashamed. After being trained about unity and reconciliation, I went to her house and asked for forgiveness. Then I shook her hand. So far, we are on good terms."

NYIRAMANA: "He killed my father and three brothers. He made these killings with other people, but he came alone to me and asked for pardon. He and a group of other offenders who had been in prison helped me build a house with a covered roof. I was afraid of him — now I have granted him pardon, things have become normal, and in my mind, I feel clear."

Godefroid Mudaheranwa, perpetrator Mukanyandwi, survivor.

MUDAHERANWA: "I burned her house. I attacked her in order to kill her and her children, but God protected them, and they escaped. When I was released from jail, if I saw her, I would run and hide. Then AMI started to provide us with training. I decided to ask her for forgiveness. To have good relationships with the person to whom you did evil deeds — we thank God."

MUKANYANDWI: "I used to hate him. When he came to my house and knelt down before me and asked for forgiveness, I was moved by his sincerity. Now, if I cry for help, he comes to rescue me. When I face any issue, I call him."

Juvenal Nzabamwita, *perpetrator* Cansilde Kampundu, *survivor*

NZABAMWITA: "I damaged and looted her property. I spent nine and a half years in jail. I had been educated to know good from evil before being released. And when I came home, I thought it would be good to approach the person to whom I did evil deeds and ask for her forgiveness. I told her that I would stand by her, with all the means at my disposal. My own father was involved in killing her children. When I learned that my parent had behaved wickedly, for that I profoundly begged her pardon, too."

KAMPUNDU: "My husband was hiding, and men hunted him down and killed him on a Tuesday. The following Tuesday, they came back and killed my two sons. I was hoping that my daughters would be saved, but then they took them to my husband's village and killed them and threw them in the latrine. I was not able to remove them from that hole. I knelt down and prayed for them, along with my younger brother, and covered the latrine with dirt. The reason I granted pardon is because I realized that I would never get back the beloved ones I had lost. I could not live a lonely life — I wondered, if I was ill, who was going to stay by my bedside, and if I was in trouble and cried for help, who was going to rescue me? I preferred to grant pardon."

Deogratias Habyarimana, *perpetrator* Cesarie Mukabutera, survivor

HABYARIMANA: "When I was still in jail, President Kagame stated that the prisoners who would plead guilty and ask pardon would be released. I was among the first ones to do this. Once I was outside, it was also necessary to ask pardon to the victim. Mother Mukabutera Caesarea could not have known I was involved in the killings of her children, but I told her what happened. When she granted me pardon, all the things in my heart that had made her look at me like a wicked man faded away."

MUKABUTERA: "Many of us had experienced the evils of war many times, and I was asking myself what I was created for. The internal voice used to tell me, "It is not fair to avenge your beloved one." It took time, but in the end, we realized that we are all Rwandans. The genocide was due to bad governance that set neighbors, brothers and sisters against one another. Now you accept, and you forgive. The person you have forgiven becomes a good neighbor. One feels peaceful and thinks well of the future."

François Ntambara, perpetrator, Epiphanie Mukamusoni, *survivor.*

NTAMBARA: "Because of the genocide perpetrated in 1994, I participated in the killing of the son of this woman. We are now members of the same group of unity and reconciliation. We share in everything; if she needs some water to drink, I fetch some for her. There is no suspicion between us, whether under sunlight or during the night. I used to have nightmares recalling the sad events I have been through, but now I can sleep peacefully. And when we are together, we are like brother and sister, no suspicion between us."

MUKAMUSONI: "He killed my child, then he came to ask me to pardon. I immediately granted it to him because he did not do it by himself — he was haunted by the devil. I was pleased by the way he testified to the crime instead of keeping it in hiding because it hurts if someone keeps hiding a crime he committed against you. Before, when I had not yet granted him pardon, he could not come close to me. I treated him like my enemy. But now, I would rather treat him like my own child."

Dominique Ndahimana, *perpetrator*, Cansilde Munganyinka, survivor.

NDAHIMANA: "The day I thought of asking pardon, I felt unburdened and relieved. I had lost my humanity because of the crime I committed, but now I am like any human being."

MUNGANYINKA: "After I was chased from my village and Dominique and others looted it, I became homeless and insane. Later, when he asked my pardon, I said: 'I have nothing to feed my children. Are you going to help raise my children? Are you going to build a house for them?' The next week, Dominique came with some survivors and former prisoners who perpetrated genocide. There were more than 50 of them, and they built my family a house. Ever since then, I have started to feel better. I was like a dry stick; now I feel peaceful in my heart, and I share this peace with my neighbors."

Laurent Nsabimana, perpetrator, Beatrice Mukarwambari, *survivor.*

NSABIMANA: "I participated in destroying her house because we took the owner for dead. The houses that remained without owners — we thought it was better to destroy them in order to get firewood. Her forgiveness proved to me that she is a person with a pure heart."

MUKARWAMBARI: "If I am not stubborn, life moves forward. When someone comes close to you without hatred, although horrible things happened, you welcome him and grant what he is looking for from you. Forgiveness equals mercy."

https://www.nytimes.com/interactive/2014/04/06/magazine/06-pieter-hugo-rwanda-portraits.html

CHAPTER 9

QUESTIONNAIRE ON FORGIVENESS

Healing toxic emotions.

The following test will help you measure the score of how high or how low is your toxicity level as far as your emotions are concerned. It's my hope that this test serves as a wake-up call to help you start a quest for optimum emotional health.

Things to know before taking the test:

1. Takes less than 45 minutes.
2. Answer truthfully and honestly, even if you don't like the answer.
3. Try not to leave any unanswered questions.
4. Take it when you are well relaxed, and try not to rush through it.

5. Note that the score analysis is based on general patterns, not a scientific scoring system. They are purely for self-awareness and self-assessment in your personal growth process.

On a scale of 0-10 with 10 being the highest, indicate at what level the following words describe you.

1. Complains

0-2

3-5

6-8

9-10

2. Feels Victimized

0-2

3-5

6-8

9-10

3. Worried

0-2

3-5

6-8

9-10

4. Bitter

0-2

3-5

6-8

9-10

5. Resentment

0-2

3-5

6-8

9-10

6. Fear of people, places or things

0-2

3-5

6-8

9-10

7. Guilt

0-2

3-5

6-8

9-10

8. Shame

0-2

3-5

6-8

9-10

9. Condemnation

0-2

3-5

6-8

9-10

10. Judgmental

0-2

3-5

6-8

9-10

11. Contempt

0-2

3-5

6-8

9-10

12. Indecisive.

0-2

3-5

6-8

9-10

13. Maligned

0-2

3-5

6-8

9-10

14. Use of Profanity/ cursing and swearing

0-2

3-5

6-8

9-10

15. Lazy, unmotivated and unproductive

0-2

3-5

6-8

9-10

16. Impatient

0-2

3-5

6-8

9-10

17. Negative.

0-2

3-5

6-8

9-10

18. Vindictive and revengeful

0-2

3-5

6-8

9-10

19. Sensitive

0-2

3-5

6-8

9-10

20. Touchy

0-2

3-5

6-8

9-10

21. Carrying a grudge

0-2

3-5

6-8

9-10

22. Insensitive

0-2

3-5

6-8

9-10

23. No compassion.

0-2

3-5

6-8

9-10

24. Mood swings

0-2

3-5

6-8

9-10

25. Restless.

0-2

3-5

6-8

9-10

26. Easily escalates in arguments

0-2

3-5

6-8

9-10

27. Suspicious and borderline paranoid

0-2

3-5

6-8

9-10

28. Not easy to trust

0-2

3-5

6-8

9-10

29. Unlikely to communicate openly and freely (more secretive and closed)

0-2

3-5

6-8

9-10

30. Loss of self-attraction

0-2

3-5

6-8

9-10

31. Self-hatred

0-2

3-5

6-8

9-10

32. Feeling Betrayed

0-2

3-5

6-8

9-10

33. Feeling Isolated

0-2

3-5

6-8

9-10

34. Strife filled

0-2

3-5

6-8

9-10

35. Toxic emotions of hurt and pain

0-2

3-5

6-8

9-10

36. Overwhelmed and fatigued all the time

0-2

3-5

6-8

9-10

37. Withdrawn and lonely

0-2

3-5

6-8

9-10

38. Disconnected from core relationships

0-2

3-5

6-8

9-10

39. Emptiness

0-2

3-5

6-8

9-10

40. Unmotivated and feeling stuck

0-2

3-5

6-8

9-10

41. Short tempered.

0-2

3-5

6-8

9-10

42. Unappreciative or feeling unappreciated

0-2

3-5

6-8

9-10

43. Sleeplessness.

0-2

3-5

6-8

9-10

44. Bored, tired and fatigued

0-2

3-5

6-8

9-10

45. Ungrateful and feels thankless

0-2

3-5

6-8

9-10

46. Suicidal and strong feelings of self-hatred

0-2

3-5

6-8

9-10

47. Unaccountable and Unsubmitted (borderline rebel/ free spirit)

0-2

3-5

6-8

9-10

48. Unconcerned even in things you'd normally care about.

0-2

3-5

6-8

9-10

49. Sad always

0-2

3-5

6-8

9-10

50. Melancholy like a slow puncture of grief

0-2

3-5

6-8

9-10

51. Overly Hesitant and chronically indecisive

0-2

3-5

6-8

9-10

52. Slander and negative about almost everything and everyone

    0-2

    3-5

    6-8

    9-10

53. Feels held back by invisible forces

    0-2

    3-5

    6-8

    9-10

54. Feeling done and unmotivated to follow the lead of others.

    0-2

    3-5

    6-8

    9-10

55. Borderline violent and losing self-restraint

    0-2

    3-5

    6-8

    9-10

56. Addicted to substances, porn, alcohol, drugs, nicotine, sugar, food or more.

0-2

3-5

6-8

9-10

57. Repeated trouble with the law, business relations, employer or spouse.

0-2

3-5

6-8

9-10

60. Extra introverted above the normal level.

0-2

3-5

6-8

9-10

61. Living in obvious denial despite the glaring warnings of others.

0-2

3-5

6-8

9-10

62. Insensitive to others feelings

0-2

3-5

6-8

9-10

63. Irrational in decisions and actions

0-2

3-5

6-8

9-10

64. Impatient and continuously quitting jobs and churches

0-2

3-5

6-8

9-10

65. Too much Self-centeredness

0-2

3-5

6-8

9-10

66. Difficulties and frustrations on every turn

0-2

3-5

6-8

9-10

67. Hard to have people gravitate to and enjoy your company.

0-2

3-5

6-8

9-10

68. Aimless.

0-2

3-5

6-8

9-10

69. Inconsistent with basic ethical and moral values

0-2

3-5

6-8

9-10

70. Pessimistic.

0-2

3-5

6-8

9-10

71. Weak willed

0-2

3-5

6-8

9-10

72. Vulnerable to past weaknesses.

0-2

3-5

6-8

9-10

73. Irritated with somebody

0-2

3-5

6-8

9-10

74. Borderline or full blown depression.

0-2

3-5

6-8

9-10

75. Sarcastic almost without trying.

0-2

3-5

6-8

9-10

HOW TO KEEP TRACK OF THE SCORES.

1. Add up the frequency of different categories. How did you score in the following categories:

   0-2: Optimum health (How many categories do you have under this?)

   3-5: Healthy enough (How many categories do you have under this?)

   6-8: Toxic (How many categories do you have under this?)

   9-10: Very toxic (How many categories do you have under this?)

Example:

0-2: Mentioned 10 times: 10/75 =13.3% Optimum Health.

3-5: Mentioned 35 times: 35/75=46.7% Healthy Enough.

6-8: Mentioned 25 times: 25/75=33.3% Toxic.

9-10: Mentioned 5 times : 5/75=6.7% Very Toxic.

2. Use the analysis below to interpret the test.

ANALYSIS

Any category where your score is 0-2 is considered very good. It is an area where you have optimum health. That is what you want for all your categories.

However, any category where your score is 3-5 and is considered average. This is not bad. However, you want to be in the range of optimum health. It means you have more room to grow. The score of 3-5 means your emotional toxicity levels are average and manageable. However, there's much room for improvement. The more you improve, the more you are able to function at your optimum level.

If your total score is 5-7 is considered toxic. It also means your general toxicity levels are above the average. This should begin to concern you. Any category where your score is between 8-10 is considered very toxic. If it's not dealt with urgently, it may become your ultimate undoing.

Don't let this score make you feel hopeless. The goal of this test is not to break you but to bless you.

3. How many categories are;

0-2 is optimum health.

3-5 is healthy enough.

6-8 is toxic.

9-10 is very toxic.

4. ASSESSMENT AND ACTION.

Take a moment to analyze and take stock of your test. What does it look like? Are there any surprises to you? Take some notes on anything that comes to your mind. Most of the things that may come to your mind have the potential to trigger your greatest changes. This is a good place to start.

If you have scores of 0-2 for any of the categories, you're doing very good in those particular areas. It's important you maintain what you are doing to ensure you remain strong in this area. Just FYI, don't overlook that there may be areas for improvement. Guard your heart and mind against whatever curve balls life may throw your way. Never feel like you've arrived. This is important to ensure you are not limiting your potential for even further growth and maturity in this area.

If you have scores of 3-5 for any of the categories, it means you're healthy enough. It's also a good thing to point out that such scores mean you're healthy enough to be functional and maintain certain levels of emotional stability. Definitely, you're are reasonably doing well in this particular area, but there is still room to grow into optimum health. Be open to finding an opportunity to explore ideas to lower your toxicity levels so that you can begin to walk in optimum emotional health.

If your scores are 6-8, you're in a toxic territory. It means that you're not doing well with your emotional health. This should begin to concern you to a point where you're willing to make some changes. Remember toxic emotions are not good for you. Also, toxic people are hurting people on the inside. It is true that hurting people hurt others.

If your score is 8-10, you are considered very toxic. This is a sign of critical levels of toxicity. That may explain why your world may be falling apart. It may also point to what is the root of the problem that has spread and spilled over into other areas of your life. You will need to explore ways of making some real drastic changes. I hope you understand it's urgent. However, you don't have to get down on yourself about these scores though. Be an optimist. The scores of 8-10 are full of opportunity to grow by making radical changes!

Note that when someone has an above average toxicity levels of 5-7 or very high toxicity levels of between 8-10, as often is the case, the individual has not fully explored the opportunities that are available to change. Many people start from there and work their way to optimum emotional health. See it as an opportunity and not an obstacle.

5. SET EMPOWERING GOALS.

Take a moment and answer the questions below:

i) *Were you honest with yourself in the way you put the score in each category ?*

ii) *What is your ideal score for each category that you commit to work to achieve in the next 1 month, 3 months, 6 months or one year?*

iii) *Which particular categories/questions do you consider to be your top priority? Pick the top 5-7 in the order of priorities.*

iv) An important thing to remember is that this is your test of life. It just shows where you are in comparison to where you can be. Indicate what scores you want for your top 5-7 categories.

6. BEGIN TO TAKE ACTION!

Commitment is key. Here and now, commit yourself to taking action. *What are the specific actions or steps that you are going to take to enhance your growth and optimum maturity in your emotional health?*

Write down what you will do.

7. LOCATE WHERE THE PROBLEM IS COMING FROM.

DIAGNOSIS: Try to zero in where the toxic emotions are coming from. Think of the following 5 obvious sources.

i) Angry with self: Do you love your body image? Do you see yourself as successful or do you feel like a failure? Have you achieved your key life goals or do you feel stuck? Are you riddled with guilt, shame, self-blame and condemnation? Could these be signs you're angry with yourself? Yes or no?

ii) Angry with God: Do you blame God for not answering your prayers? Do you feel let down and hurt by church? Have you given up on waiting and believing again? Do you have unresolved debates on why bad things happen to you? Could this mean that you are angry with God? Yes or no?

iii) Angry with other person(s): Think of 3 to 5 people that constantly drive you crazy right now. Think of spouses, workmates, friends, business partners, neighbors, and relatives. If there is anyone that comes to your mind right now, then it is evident you are angry with someone. That could be the source of your toxic emotions. Is there a person(s)? Yes or no?

iv) Root of bitterness: The root of bitterness comes from prolonged periods of walking and living with unforgiveness. Have you held a grudge for a prolonged period of time? This could mean anywhere from one day to weeks, months or years. Most likely you will see a root of bitterness based on how long you have not walked in forgiveness. Is it true you've carried a lot of bitter emotions for some time? Yes or no?

v) Trauma: Is there an event that has taken place in your life which left you in fear, dread, anxiety and feeling the wind knocked out of you. Here are some common causes of trauma. Diagnosis of an incurable disease, a near death experience, extreme childhood experiences, violence, blow of death of a loved one, divorce, natural catastrophe, bankruptcy, betrayal or a major loss. Any extreme life experience that lacks love, joy, and peace; has the potential of being a traumatic experience.

Trauma is a spirit of fear. It is due to extreme and dramatic negative impact that shatters the soul and leaves someone broken into a million pieces. During trauma, it's a vulnerable time. Many traumatic issues gain strength when they affect us in childhood. They form a stronghold of trauma. Obviously, trauma can become an open door for the entrance of demonic spirits and toxic emotions. It's those negative effects that tend to rule over our souls and minds. Do you see anything that mirrors the above description? Yes or no?

8. You're on your way to victory! Now that you have the right tools, begin to focus on dealing with it. Always remember, hurting people hurt others. The baggage of the hurt can destroy a great marriage and ruin friendship.

Get a grip on it. That's why I designed a 40-day accountability class to help you lower your toxicity levels. It will immediately affect the quality of your life. As your mentor, I want to walk you out into a path of freedom.

PRAYER OF FORGIVENESS

Father God, in the name of Jesus, I ask you to forgive me for all my sins, past, present and future. Cleanse me from all my failings. Anything sinful that has come between us, cleanse it in Jesus name. Today, I declare that I have peace with God. My sins are forgiven, and I am loved.

I also repent for being angry with you. My anger has been because I don't know you as I should. But I believe you're a good God. You are not the author of evil. Every good and perfect gift comes from you. You're a good father. I lay down my pride. I let go of my anger against you. I receive forgiveness, peace, and reconciliation with you.

I receive you in my life. Be my Lord and Savior. Write my name in the book of life. Give me a new beginning.

My vertical relationship with you is now healed.

Now I turn my attention to my horizontal relationships with others. I now forgive all who have wronged me. Everything in my past, present, and future. All the people that have offended me. I name them one by one (name all until you are done). I forgive them. Those that I have offended (name them all), I also forgive them in the name of Jesus Christ. I declare that all my relationships are healed and freed from all pain.

I now pray for myself. I forgive myself of perfectionism, self-hatred, guilt, shame, blame, and condemnation. I accept myself as I am. I'm fearfully and wonderfully made. I'm loved and not condemned. I'm very special in his eyes.

Today, I proclaim all the blessings of heaven on my life and on the lives of my loved ones. My soul is free. My emotions are healed and whole again. My mind is renewed. My body is healed. My heart is at peace. Depression, anxiety, fear, trauma, bitterness, anger, resentment, jealousy and all toxic emotions are now healed in Jesus name.

I'm a new creation. I have a new life. It's a new day. It's a new beginning. I walk in love. I am functional and perform in optimum capacity.

I proclaim my total freedom!

CONCLUSION

Lord, Make us instruments of your peace,

Where there is hatred, let your love increase

Lord, make us instruments of your peace,

Walls of pride and prejudice shall cease

When we are your instruments of peace.

Where there is hatred, we will show his love

Where there is injury, we will never judge

Where there is striving, we will speak his peace

To the millions crying for release,

We will be his instruments of peace

Lord, Make us instruments of your peace,

Where there is hatred, let your love increase

Lord, make us instruments of your peace,

Walls of pride and prejudice shall cease

When we are your instruments of peace.

Where there is blindness, we will pray for sight
where there is darkness, we will shine his light
Where there is sadness, we will bear their grief
To the millions crying for relief,
We will be your instruments of peace

(Instruments Of Your Peace. Deny Dearman and Kirk Dearman)

ENROLL IN MY 40 DAYS
OF FORGIVENESS THERAPY

Name

Email

Phone number

What are 3-5 things that are pressing hard on you right now?

APPENDIX

ABOUT THE AUTHOR

D r. Charles is an apostle to the nations who has traveled around the world conducting healing and deliverance crusades since 1991. In stadiums, arenas, and churches, thousands have been saved and set free by the power of God. The lame walk, the blind see and the deaf hear as God's miraculous power is released to minister to the desperate needs of humanity.

As a speaker, author and trainer, Dr. Charles has traveled widely for seminars and conferences in leadership development and capacity building in over 23 nations in United States, Europe, South America, Asia, Australia, Canada, and Africa.

Dr. Charles is also an intercessor and a spiritual father whose main goal is to mentor people to help them fulfill their destiny in God. He is the lead pastor of International Outreach Church, a growing multi-faceted/multi-racial church in the Twin Cities MN, USA.

He is the President of the Institute of Leadership and Mentorship (ILM). He holds a Bachelors Degree in Education, a Master Degree in Leadership and 2 Honorary Doctorate Degrees in Humanities and International Relations. Dr. Charles is passionate about developing leaders and building capacity in organizations. He is an example of global leadership as he operates as a Golden Rule Goodwill Ambassador, a mentor, speaker, and leader.

Dr. Charles is a recipient of the prestigious Global Leadership Award as well as an appointed World Civility Ambassador.

He has produced numerous training materials and is also regularly heard in the State of Minnesota by live stream, media platforms, and training schools.

As a husband and a father of 5, Dr. Charles loves to coach soccer and inspire others. He enjoys watching documentaries and competitive sports games.

For more information, visit www.experienceioc.com, or www.ILMedu.com

WHAT OTHERS ARE SAYING ABOUT DR. CHARLES.

IChange nations™ awarded Dr. Charles Karuku with the Global Leadership Award for his outstanding qualities as a global leader and his creative leadership ideas that are changing lives around the world. Ambassador Rivers says, *"It is always a privilege to honor a man like Dr. Charles Karuku. His creativity and mentorship literally help people and organizations become better. The value of life is a large part of the philosophy of IChange Nations™, and Dr. Charles is truly an example of outstanding leadership, and by his actions, it is evident that he believes every life is valuable."*

Dr. Clyde Rivers
President iChange Nations.

"Charles Karuku is an able leader with a reputation, acumen, and skills in directing and developing leaders. The Institute of Leadership and Mentorship has been highly successful in producing leaders who were personally trained by Charles and are able to effectively apply their skills learned during their training.

I have been consistently impressed with Charles innate understanding and knowledge base in regards to abilities to apply leadership skills to many environments, specifically related to business matters. Charles has come to be my mentor and friend. I have come to fully appreciate and rely on his feedback and recommendations as applied to my business. I own 3 clinics in the Twin Cities area with a team of 5 doctors,8 massage therapists and a staff of more than 20 people. I can, without reservation, give Charles Karuku the highest recommendation personally and professionally with respect to his ethical approaches and conduct as he develops and mentors future leaders."

Dr. R.A. Hills

Founder and President

Institute of Orthopedics & Chiropractic

Edina MN, USA.

"Charles is a True Mentor & a very diversified leader. He has been guiding me in all aspects of my life both personal and business. He certainly refined my mindset and the way I used to approach things."

S. Jalal
CEO
i-Invest Properties
Private Lending Consultants.
North American Real Estate & Business Investors,
Toronto Canada.

"Charles Karuku is a very vibrant person. I believe that God has raised him in this time with a special and powerful message for all nations around the world. He is an example in his deep faith, arduous work, and dedication. He is a true leader. His teaching and leadership training has changed my life. I am grateful to God for his life and family."

G. I. Miranda Vicente.
Human Rights Lawyer and environmental
conservationist, Mexico, City, Mexico

"Dr. Charles experience incorporates high qualities of ethics, confidentiality and a deep sense of justice, honor, and understanding of people.He is an avid proponent for youth empowerment, and always strives to represent God's ideals in creating the environment for their holistic development. I, therefore, happily and unhesitatingly take this opportunity to present Dr. Charles Karuku Founder and President of ILM."

Senator Hon. Dr. Winston Garraway

Minister of State, Prime Minister's Ministry

In charge of Information and Disaster Management

in the nation of Grenada.

"Dr. Charles and Lindsey lead a fantastic team of committed leaders who show by their example what it is to live the life of servanthood. You cannot be around them without sensing the heart and passion for the world and for the people. Their practical and spiritual advice will set you on the right course and teach you leadership through sacrifice."

Expecting the best,

Senator Dan Hall.

"Dr. Charles Karuku is a man of wisdom, integrity, revelation, and passion for building others and raising up leaders. I highly recommend the Institute of Leadership and Mentorship - a new paradigm of leadership education, training, mentorship, and impartation with tangible results."

Dr. James Rene Pastor, Spiritual Growth,
Higher Vision Church Prof. Messenger College

Made in the USA
Monee, IL
07 March 2021

62170530R00098